I0484076

# SELF INFLICTED

## The 7 Deadly Mistakes Of Operating A Small Business

*"It ain't what you don't know that gets you into trouble.
It's what you know for sure that just ain't so."*

~ Mark Twain

This book was printed in the United States

Mermaid Green Publishing
1410 Brunson Court
Cary, North Carolina 2751
www.mermaidgreen.com

Some images and illustration used under license
from: Jupiterimages Corporation ©2009
23 Old Kings Highway South
Darien, CT 06820
www.clipart.com

# Other Titles By Fred Tutwiler

All titles are published by Mermaid Green Publications and are available on Amazon.com

## Breaking Your MEGAgiNormous Rules
*The rules you live by, why they keep you stuck and what you can do about it*

## The Ultimate Gas Saver's Guide
*Low Cost/No Cost tips and techniques to use less gas, save money and help the environment*

## The Ultimate College Care Package Guide
*Stay in touch, be supportive and make life easier for the new college student in your life.*

## Best Darn Cruising Tips EVER!
*The best tips EVER to help get you ready to make the absolute most of your Caribbean cruise.*

# Table Of Contents

## The Dinosaur's Tail
*(A story about Unintentional Living)*

Long, long ago, in the Land Before Time, there lived a gentle giant, which we know today as a Brontosaurus. These were the largest land

animals ever, growing as tall as 80 feet and weighing 35 tons.  Unlike many of his fellow prehistoric partners, like Tyrannosaurus and Stegosaurus, Brontosaurus was a total plant eater.  He would wander with his friends and family through the country side (which we now call Montana, Colorado and Utah) peacefully nibbling the tender, juicy tops of tall trees.  He was completely non-aggressive. Brontosaurus had a VERY small head, and

# VE-E-E-E-E-Ery small

brain.  And when he was munching away, minding his own Bronto-business he didn't pay much attention to what was going on around him. *(munch, munch)*

Indeed, even if he noticed other species acting up and fighting with each other, he didn't get involved. And, interestingly enough, due to his enormous size, and his HUGE TAIL even the meanest meat-eaters often stayed away from Bronto-burgers.

*So, one would think that this quiet, tolerant species would just thrive in the green forests of the North American west.*

But, our pea-brained friends had <u>one</u> <u>unfortunate practice,</u>
and it proved to be…

## …their greatest enemy

You see, as they leisurely strolled through the country-side snacking and nibbling, (which they had to do a lot of to keep themselves fed), their

### ENORMOUS TAILS,

*(sometimes 100 feet long and weighing 5 tons!)* ,

wagged contentedly behind them (kind of like a big ol' cat). Nothing wrong with that, unless you happen to be a *tree* in the way of the contented wag.

Yep, as our peaceful throng of Bronto-munchers grazed through the forest, they destroyed pretty much everything behind them.

## SMASH!!!  CRASH!!!

# *TIMBE-E-E-E-E-ER!!!*

Well, there goes tomorrow's snack,

### and next <u>year's</u> snack as well.

Unaware of **THE IMPACT** of their actions, they could only move on, searching for nourishment elsewhere. They were unable to comprehend what was happening. Through no fault of their own, they were **UNAWARE OF THE**

**IMPACT** of their contentedly wagging tails, and could do nothing about it. You could say that they had all their attention on themselves. They weren't selfish or mean. They were

### Simply UNAWARE OF THE IMPACT OF THEIR ACTIONS.

## *And so…*

*…the most kindly of all the prehistoric armor-plated giants effectively destroyed its own options, killing off itself and its family, ruining the land for many others simply because it was*

# UNAWARE OF THE IMPACT OF ITS ACTIONS.

Humans are a lot like the kindly Brontosaurus. Mostly content to "mind our own business" (that's code for do what works for us), we go through life, picking and choosing what we will do, worried only about where our next "meal" (i.e., excitement, love, security, fun, excuse, VICTORY) is coming from, often paying very little attention to what disruption we leave behind.

It's kind of funny when you think about it.

 Here we highly-evolved humans are with this big brain, 100 times the size of a Bronto-dummy, but we're no more aware of the chaos we apathetically cause around us then those prehistoric lizards.

## *(sigh. Do you think it's worth noting that those lizards are now EXTINCT??!!)*

*Operating a small business is a pain-in-the-neck, thankless, sometimes lonely, often desperate, never fully appreciated journey, full of bad days, bad dudes, hidden agendas, low pay and no vacations.*

*Being your own boss is a roller-coaster ride of headaches, triumphs, frustrations and rewards, which isn't always pretty.*

*But then, neither is making sausage.*

**Two More Distinctions We'll Be Using In This Book**

*Reprinted with permission from Breaking Your MEGAgiNormous Rules. These apply everywhere in your life, but they are REALLY powerful in your small business environmernt.*

## THE HAIRBALL

> *hair ball: n., a magnificent metaphor introduced by Gordon MacKenzie in his wonderful book "Orbiting the Giant Hairball: A Corporate Fool's Guide to Surviving with Grace"*

### What Is A Hairball?

We've all heard of hairballs. You know those disgusting masses of gunk and matted hair that a cat coughs up from time to time. As yucky as it is, it didn't start out that way.

The metaphor relies on the well-known practice of a cat cleaning itself, which results in swallowing a lot of hairs. A *hairball* begins with two hairs uniting, then another, then another, and finally where there altogether different from the individual hairs that make it up.

As the hairball gets bigger, it develops its own gravity, pulling more and more hairs into it, becoming bigger all the time. Eventually, the purpose of the hairball is to preserve and expand itself.

Each individual hair is no big deal. But when you accumulate *thousands* of hairs together, all co-mingled and packed tight, you get a mass of something. That mass doesn't just sit benignly in a dark place until you hack it up and get rid of it. Oh NO! It takes on a life of its own.

No single conclusion or decision you make *(hair)* is all that important, but the collection of them all together is a force to be reckoned with. It becomes your FUTURE.

Over time, there is little resemblance between <u>why</u> you arrived at a particular conclusion and how the hairball eventually incorporates it.

> **You can't logic your way out of a conclusion that you didn't logic your way into in the first place.**

Furthermore, even though you practically <u>never</u> remember WHY you came to a particular conclusion, you NEVER forget the conclusion itself. You are forever after defined by it to varying degrees, <u>even if it no longer applies to you, or to the circumstances you are in now.</u>

Where your business is concerned, you didn't start accumulating hairs the day you started your business. You brought your own hairball to the party. Over time, you added THOUSANDS of hairs from your ongoing business activities, and the resulting hairball co-mingled everything into a newer, more complicated hairball that now dictates your behavior in your business AND your life.

Trying to <u>change</u> a single conclusion is like trying to remove a single hair from that yucky mass the cat coughs up. As such, it is mostly futile. Unfortunately, you can't logic your way out of a conclusion that you didn't logic your way into in the first place! (Sigh).

**THE COHERENCE FACTOR**

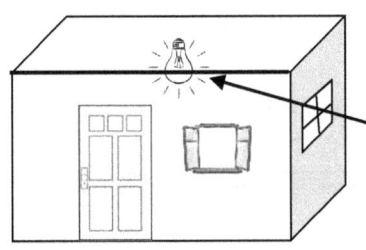

Imagine that you're standing in a room and hanging from the ceiling in the middle of the room is a single bare 60-watt incandescent light bulb. If this were the only light in the room, you might be able to see fairly well right under it, but you would quickly walk into darkness as you approached the corners of the room.

This 60-watt light bulb produces energy in the form of light waves, that spread out from the filament moving in all directions at the same time.

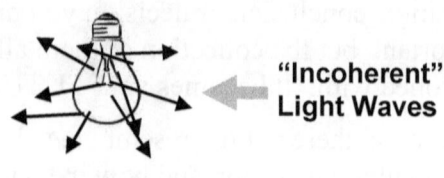

"Incoherent" Light Waves

This disorganized distribution of light energy causes the waves to disperse randomly, some bumping into each other, others going off in random directions. Scientists call this "incoherent" light. The light waves work against each other, generating heat and light.

It is useful that a light bulb works this way because it allows us to see in the dark. Unfortunately, it wastes a lot of energy in the form of heat.

MIRROR

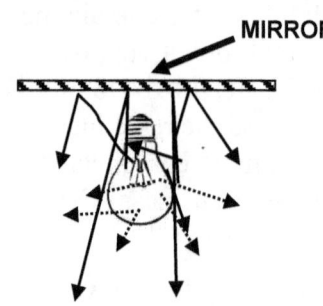

If you were to place a mirror on the ceiling, more light would be directed downward. Adding more mirrors around the bulb, you would eventually end up with a spotlight effect in which all of the light's energy was directed at a single point.

Logically, that single point would be much brighter – exponentially brighter – even though <u>you did not increase the amount of light energy.</u>

If you continued this mirroring process far enough, eventually the light waves would become ordered and focused, moving together in the same direction at the same time. In other words, the light energy would become "coherent". The ultimate example of coherent light is a laser beam.

"Coherent" Light Waves

The ultimate light beam focus machine -

A Laser Beam

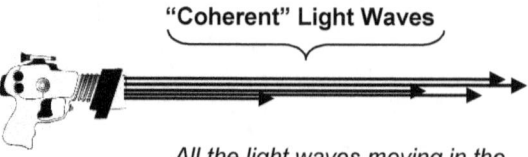

*All the light waves moving in the same direction at the same time*

While 60-watts of incoherent light (the light bulb) will barely light up a single room, 60-watts of coherent light (the laser beam) is capable of burning a hole all the way through the sun, 90,000,000 miles away!  The same 60 watts of energy!

## The Coherence Factor And Your Business

In the same way that *light waves* can be incoherent, so can the *actions* you take in your business. And it has the same effect. Allowing yourself to pursue multiple projects, being inconsistent in your actions and policies, or making frequent course corrections, will scatter your attention in all different directions. Your effectiveness will suffer. You will end up with a lot of activity ("heat and light"), but you will also waste a lot of energy. Worse still, you will interrupt any momentum you have going in your business.

If you stick with the things you are already good at, and if you only take on commitments that you can deliver now, you focus your resources and your energy, like the mirrors focus light waves.

Every action you take is a "light wave". Every conversation, every customer interaction, every business transaction, every choice you make, are all light waves. When those waves are random and unintentional, you waste valuable time and resources. When you *consciously* take actions in a focused way, you unleash the power of coherence in your business.  Even limited resources can have an amazing effect if they are utilized coherently.

---

**60 Watt Bulb Lights Up A Room**

Or

**60-watt Laser Beam Burns A Hole Through The Sun
90,000,000 Million Miles Away**

**SAME ENERGY**

**WAY MORE COHERENCE**

**CHOOSE**

---

The best description I ever heard about people who start their own business is that they are

> *egomaniacs embarking on a mission that*
> *they mistakenly believe they understand.*

A bit harsh maybe, but not far from the truth. Those of us who have decided to step outside the secure mainstream and undertake this adventure – an adventure that has very little statistical chance of succeeding - must indeed have healthy egos. And I'm certain that all of us feel we know what we are doing, or at least we did when we began.

To travel the road of the small business owner is to visit a path that is strewn recklessly with the forgotten carcasses of those millions who came before. Less than 10% of us will achieve our ultimate objectives. The rest will only live on in the minds of grumbling creditors and smiling competitors.

## Why Do So Many Small Businesses Fail

Clearly, it's not enough to give it your best shot, or to try really hard. It's not enough to have a good plan and smart tactics, or to be honest. If that were the case, 90% of small businesses would succeed. But the stats show just the opposite. So what is it?

Self-Inflicted is not be a checklist of "How To Succeed In Business". It's actually more basic than that. You see, even if you obsess with doing the RIGHT things

### it's more important to avoid doing the WRONG things!

If you make enough mistakes, it simply won't matter how much other stuff you do right. You'll never have the chance to enjoy the fruits of your *right-ness*. In small businesses, the impact of doing the right things takes times, sometimes a couple of years. But, the impact of mistakes can be felt immediately.

Many of the mistakes identified in this book apply to any size business.  But this book focuses on *small businesses* because they have a real urgency to identify and avoid the very mistakes we'll be looking at.

## Who This Book Is Intended For

According to the U.S. Department of Labor Statistics, a small business is defined by two criteria:

1.  Fewer than 500 employees

2.  Less than $7 Million in profit annually. That is <u>profit</u>, not <u>revenues</u>.  To generate $7 million in profits, a typical business needs to generate $40 - $50 million in revenues.

---

### A Few Interesting Stats About Small Businesses

- There are 28 million small businesses in the U.S.

- 95% of small business have 10 or fewer employees.

- Over 60% of all small business generate revenues of *less than $50,000 per year.*

- 95% have revenues of less than $300K

- About 5% of all small businesses in the U.S. generate almost as much revenue as the other 95% combined.

**Approximately $1.1 Trillion in Annual Revenues**

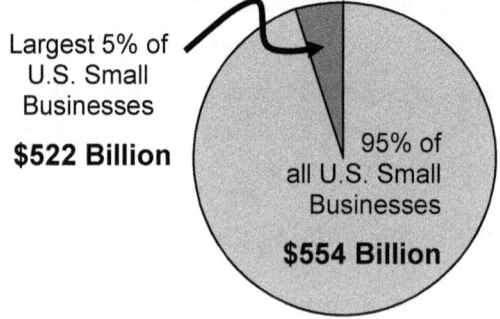

Largest 5% of U.S. Small Businesses

**$522 Billion**

95% of all U.S. Small Businesses

**$554 Billion**

Of these 28 million small businesses,

**95% will cease to operate before the end of their 3<sup>rd</sup> year**

---

**Why is this important to you?**

Here's the take-away – 95% of U.S. small business have 10 or fewer employees and net $300K or less per year.

The other 5% include people who have from 10 – 500 employees and net $300K - $7 Million per year. Unless you are part of that 5%, YOU cannot afford to do things the way they do it.

Said another way,

> *The reality of the 5% is <u>substantially different</u> than the reality of the 95%.*

There are a lot of folks out there who love to TALK about the importance of small businesses, and how much they adore the courage and grit it takes to run a small businesses (blah, blah, blah).

> **They are NOT talking about YOU. They are talking about the 5%.**

To most of the business world, YOU (i.e., the 95%) are a revenue stream, or a voting block. <u>Nothing more.</u>

- Government agencies (state and federal) will NOT implement policies that benefit you. You are too busy running your business to spend your time and money on getting people elected. So, you don't really matter in the political arena.

- Organizations that profess to represent you (Chambers of Commerce, National Federation of Independent Businesses, etc) will be happy to take you membership fees, but they will NOT lobby for your interests.

- Banks will spend millions of dollars advertising how wonderful they are for small business clients, but what they're really interested in is the fees they get to charge you, especially the BILLIONS of dollars in NSF fees they're going to collect from you every year. But they will NOT
  - ◆ Make it easier for you to borrow money
  - ◆ Give you lower fees

- ◆ Extend lines of credit
- ◆ Give back some of those BILLIONS of dollars in NSF fees they are going to collect from you for doing absolutely nothing.

### It's NOT A Level Playing Field - Get Over It!

Whatever romantic notions you have about how much America loves the entrepreneur spirit, the reality is – nobody has your back!

While it may be true that our economic culture relies on small businesses for its health, the dominant forces that rule that culture - financial, market penetration and political - still weigh heavily in favor of that 5%.

Don't go getting depressed or indignant about that, it's just part of the game we CHOOSE to play.

---

**It is NOT a problem that there are different rules for the 95% than those that apply to the 5%.**

**It IS a problem if you don't understand that basic reality.**

---

### The Invisible Box - Paradigms

Whether we are aware of it or not, we all have a particular way of looking at the world, especially as it relates to our business. All of our actions are consistent with that view. We all operate our businesses, and our lives, inside a "box" of rules, expectations and guidelines.

*__All__ of our business strategies and tactics are based on which __paradigms__ of thinking we embrace.*

A paradigm is a set of rules and regulations (written or unwritten) that dictate our basic way of perceiving, thinking, valuing, and doing things. All of our paradigms together make up our view of reality.

# Paradigm =

*Something we unquestionably accept as being true*

*Things we take for granted*

*Things that are so obvious they "go without saying"*

Not surprisingly, many other people and organizations, perhaps everyone we know, shares paradigms similar to ours. In fact, we may even disrespect, or be suspicious of, those people who do not operate consistent with our paradigm. You will probably notice that, in most areas of your life, you gravitate toward those people whose paradigms match up with yours.

## Typical Paradigms About Business And Work

- Monday-Friday work week
- Job stability
- Christmas holidays
- Health insurance
- Retirement
- Vacations

The list, of course, is endless. Paradigms <u>can</u> be a good thing, but not all prevailing "business" paradigms work for the SMALL business.

## Why Do Paradigms Matter So Much?

Our paradigms are invisible to us. They are *reality*. And therefore, many of the *mistakes* we make will also be invisible to us. Said another way, we are often UNAWARE of the consequences of our actions.

After all, we would never INTENTIONALLY put our business at risk. So, if we do end up making a mistake, it's probably because *we didn't know it was a mistake*.

And why do we not know something is a mistake? Because our business paradigms don't tell us. If they did, we wouldn't make the mistake!

Going along with some strategy or way of doing things just because that's what everyone else is doing is a risky (deadly?) way to operate your business

### A Relevant Piece of History

After the Wright Brothers proved that manned flight was possible in 1903, industry was reluctant to embrace this potential new form of travel and shipping It was due to WWI, and the military's appetite for better fighting advantages, that flight technology advanced at all in the 15 years after 1903.

Surprisingly, even after such success in the war, the paradigm of flight did not immediately take hold in the US. Most pilots returning home from the war could only find work as carnival attractions or crop dusters. Flight did not become a viable form of transportation until 1926, when the US Postal Service decided to use surplus war machinery to deliver the mail.

> *Reasonable business men and speculators simply could not envision that the prevailing modes of transportation (locomotives and ships) were soon to be overshadowed by the new paradigm of flight.*

The demise of the powerful railroad companies, who contributed so much to the expansion and growth of America at the turn of the century, was due to their inability to see the difference between the paradigm of "transportation" versus the paradigm of "railroads". Sounds like a pretty big mistake, don't you think?

# A Few Other "Obvious Facts" From Smart People

"There is no reason anyone would want a computer in their home." - *Ken Olson, president, chairman and founder of Digital Equipment Corp., 1977.*

"This 'telephone' has too many shortcomings to be seriously considered as a means of communication. The device is inherently of no value to us." - *Western Union internal memo, 1876.*

"Drill for oil? You mean drill into the ground to try and find oil? You're crazy." - *Water well drillers who were asked by Edwin L. Drake to help him drill for oil in 1859.*

"Television won't be able to hold onto any market it captures after the first six months. People will soon get tired of staring at a plywood box every night." - *Darryl F Zanuck, Hollywood producer and movie executive, 1946.*

"The horse is here to stay, but the automobile is only a novelty." - *President of Michigan Savings Bank, 1903, advising Henry Ford's lawyer not to invest in the Ford Motor Company.*

"When the Paris Exhibition closes, electric light will close with it and no more be heard of." - *Erasmus Wilson, professor at Oxford University, 1878.*

## You Might Even Think They're True.

## "Obvious Facts" That Are ALWAYS Wrong For The 95%

- Money = success
- Do whatever it takes to get your foot in the door
- Sell now, figure out how to deliver later
- You gotta spend money to make money
- Employees are a necessary problem. It's cheaper or easier to use friends or family
- Customer Service is a good idea, but not essential
- You're not big enough to justify a quality control program
- It's worth whatever it takes in the short term. You'll get your payout when the ship comes in

> *GREAT NEWS! The mistakes of small businesses owners are not mysterious or unique to our circumstances. WE'RE ALL MAKING THE SAME ONES. We can learn from that!*

In a small business, <u>every</u> decision is potentially critical. Adding to the pressure is the fact that many of those decisions, especially the REALLY important ones, usually deal with a new situation.

And quite often, you don't have the time or the resources to fully enlighten yourself, assuming there is a light available. The result is that you are often forced to fly by the seat of your pants. It may not be true at all that entrepreneurs *like* to fly by the seat of their pants as much as it is true that they <u>must</u> do that to get anything done.

For whatever reason, quick and decisive action is the norm in the small business world, and unfortunately that often means uninformed action, which almost always leads to mistakes.

In the upcoming pages we are going to discuss the deadliest of those mistakes, and how not to make them. Your mission, should you decide to accept it, is to find a way to get through the traps, clear the hurdles, endure the hardship and come out with your dignity, your financial well-being and your sense of humor intact.

> *If it was easy, everybody would do it, and then you'd be just another examiner at the driver's license office.*

## CRITICALLY IMPORTANT TURTHS FOR THE 95%

Number 1 -   Don't waste money on anything.

Number 2 -   involve yourself <u>only</u> in situations that you can control, then do so with honesty and integrity.

Number 3 -   Everything you want in life, that you don't now possess, is either owned by, or controlled by, another *human being*. Operate accordingly.

# THE DEADLY MISTAKES

**"If winning was simply a matter of discipline, Army and Navy would win the National Championship every year"**
*Bobby Bowden, Head Football Coach, Florida State University*

i\If succeeding in a small business was simply a matter of doing the things one is taught in business school, everyone who got a business degree would be a successful business owner.

About 30 years ago, Mark McCormack wrote a very good book titled *What They Don't Teach You At Harvard Business School.* McCormack was the founder and chairman of International Management Group, now IMGWorld, an international mega-sports agency that represented golf and tennis professionals such as Arnold Palmer, Jack Nicholas and Tiger Woods.

The point of his book was to show how he applied "street-smart" insights as opposed to Harvard Business School principles. Drawing on dozens of examples from his business experience, McCormack illustrated the flaws in the prevailing conventional thinking (paradigms).

But even McCormack's well-done points came from a *corporate* paradigm. They came from a business world that most of us dream of achieving, but simply aren't there. Yes, we aspire to that goal, and some of us might get there. But, our challenge is more immediate, and lots riskier. If you had read McCormack's book, as millions of people did, and then relied on its points to guide your business, you would take actions on building your company like it was a multi-million-dollar international company.

As intriguing as McCormack's ideas are, they would saddle your business with lots of beta spending. That approach only works if you've got lots of money to back you up. Most small businesses can't afford the luxury of making back huge loses over time.

> *Our stock-holders don't cut our bonuses when we lose the farm. They repo our cars and shut off our utilities!*

## Wasting Money: Avoiding The Slot Machine Paradigm

> YES. There IS a reason this is the <u>first topic</u> on the list of DEADLY MISTAKES!

> *The <u>Slot Machine Paradigm</u> says "If you let yourself get sucked in a quarter at a time, you'll pay long after someone else has won the jackpot."*

Every business idea that was ever conceived, no matter how big or small, is a hostage to money to some degree. And, it simply does not matter how wonderful your business idea is if you can't afford to implement it in a timely fashion.

As boring as it is talking about how you spend your money, it is the talk that must happen. You need to be able to spend money on the things your business needs in a timely manner. And you can't do that if you don't have enough money when you need it.

There are so many ways that you can undermine your success by not managing your money properly that it is hard to know where to start. To begin with, you should have a hard, fast philosophy that says,

### "Don't Waste a Single Penny! EVER!"

Okay, now breathe. For starters, let's accept the fact that spending mistakes are as much a part of running a small business as long workdays. So, we don't want to throw the baby out with the bathwater. Suck it up. Don't complain. That's just part of the messy deal you bought into.

**But, you MUST train yourself to stop adding to the mess unnecessarily!**

You are going to make decisions about spending money that will drive you up a wall. Not because you are incompetent or aren't paying attention. But because there is a lo-o-ong learning curve.

> **It takes time to get good at making wise spending decisions. They are a product of experience, not intuition.**

Unfortunately, this experience usually comes with a hefty price tag, the learning curve takes time, and the tuition payment comes due before the lesson is learned, DANG!

Spending decisions that end up wasting money are either due to:

- Incomplete/wrong information, and/or
- Having too much enthusiasm for the particular expenditure

In either case, one's ability to make an objective decision is hindered.

**Complicating the process is the fact that we usually rely on the very people who are trying to get us to spend money as our primary source for information on the wisdom of spending that money.**

> *When was the last time an advertisement salesperson tried to convince you NOT to advertise in their medium?*

### "BS" Spending

Most wasteful spending decisions fall into two broad categories (paradigms), the "Buying Success" category, and the "Best Scenario" category. Keep in mind, a spending decision that is completely needed and legitimate can go completely off the rails if it gets corrupted by either of these paradigms.

## Buying Success

In the first case, we succumb to the myth that in order to be successful you have to *appear* successful. We become seduced by popular fantasies like:

- You gotta look GOOD, Baby!", and
- "You have to spend money to make money", and
- "If your not growing you're backing up" and
- "Go big or stay home"

I have a friend who took on a $500/month lease payment for a tricked-out shiny, king-cab 4-wheel drive-pick up truck because he had convinced himself that customers wouldn't want to hire a building contractor that wasn't successful. Just sayin'...

## Best Scenario

In the second case we spend money because we have convinced ourselves (or we let some else convince us) that a complex chain of events will fall magically into place and we will be rewarded with more business than we can handle. You know,

*"If we get just 30 orders from this advertisement, and each order averages $167.00, and if we can ship all of them within 60 days, then the ad will pay for itself before we have to come up with the money to pay for the ad!"*

Appropriately enough, each of these categories can be shortened to a more common acronym, "BS". 'Nuff said!

---

### *Welcome To The "Dough-Zone"*

*You know that mysterious phenomenon when you "lose" a sock in the dryer? It is explained by the existence of the "Toe-Zone", a cosmic netherworld where socks go to ... do whatever solo socks do.*

*It's the same place your money goes when you don't pay attention to how you spend it. And, just like that lost sock, you never get your money back.*

---

### If You Don't Spend Money, You Can't Waste It!

> **A BIG LIE:  You have to spend money to make money!**

No matter what the popular belief may be,

> *You are much more likely to hurt your business by spending money badly, than by not spending money that might help you.*

No doubt, there are many essential priorities that require you to spend money.  But we're not talking about such things as rent and utilities and insurance, at least not in this chapter.  And there are plenty of very good reasons to spend money on things that are risky. But, as a small business, you can't afford to waste money.

**Money gets wasted when it is spent for something that does not make a direct, positive contribution to our business.**

Regardless of what you thought was going to happen when you spent it, if it ends up being a bad move, then it was a waste and you would have been better off not spending it.  The negative effect of this is exponentially increased when you waste money that you don't have, such as when you buy advertising or lease a piece of equipment expecting (or needing) the purchase to pay for itself in the near future to justify the spending.

"Hold on!", you say.

"Every time I spend money I'm trying to make a positive contribution to my business.  But you can't always know in advance if it's going to work out that way."

True enough.

"And besides", you add, "making mistakes is part of the process. Every decision is a gamble.  How can anyone know for sure that a decision is the right one?"

Good question.  Lucky you are reading this book because it is going to show you how to find the answer.

## MERLIN'S SPENDING GRAPH

### A Quick, Easy Way To Find Out If You Should Make A Particular Spending Decision BEFORE You Make It.

*In the Tales of King Arthur's Knights of The Round Table, Merlin was Arthur's confidant and personal sorcerer. Merlin's secret was that he lived life in <u>reverse</u> of everyone else. He lived from the future back into the present. He already knew what was likely to happen before it happened. This graph will tell you what is likely to happen BEFORE you spend your money.*

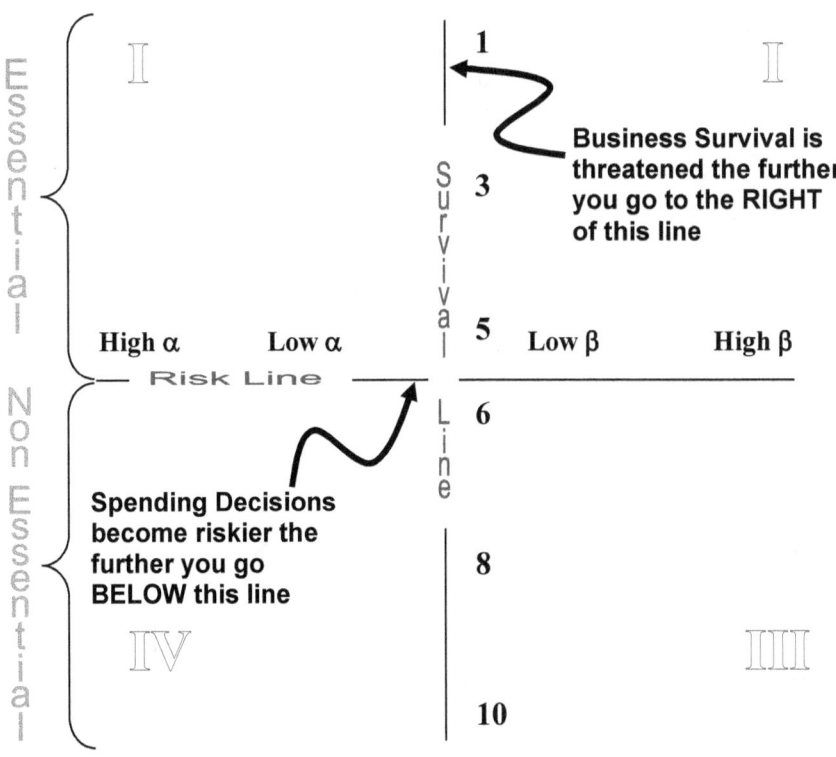

**Merlin's Spending Graph – a roadmap to smarter spending.**

| THE SURVIVAL LINE<br>What Are You Spending Your Money <u>On</u>? | |
|---|---|
| The vertical line plots the PRIORITY of a spending decision. | |
| | **Description of Priority** |
| **1** | Critical to the company's survival. For example, you probably need some kind of telephone to conduct business, so it is a #1 priority. |
| **3** | *Not essential for survival*, but it *is essential for efficient operation* of your business. For example, you may not need a computer to survive, but if you are not able to keep track of your receivables in a timely fashion, it could be a very wise purchase. |
| **5** | Necessary for the <u>profitable</u>, <u>controlled</u> <u>expansion</u> of your business. After all, in even the best cases, you will need to expand your customer base to keep up with increased costs and the inevitable attrition of old customers. The operative words here are ***profitable*** and ***controlled***. |
| **7** | Primarily intended to generate, or accommodate, significant growth, such as, opening up a second location to increase access to your product or service. |
| **10** | Perks *(Perquisite- something you do just because you want to)*. If you decide to replace all your office furniture with hand-carved teak, you might convince yourself that you need to do it to make a good impression (see "Buying Success" above), but there's a REALLY good chance that you just want high-class furniture in your office. |

And, by the way, THERE'S NOTHING WRONG WITH SPENDING MONEY ON #10 PRIORITIES

Just be sure you are NOT spending money on a #10 Priority when you have unpaid bills for items that are #1 or #3 Priorities.

## Which Brings Us To The Risk Line.

| THE RISK LINE<br>What <u>Money</u> Are You Spending? | |
| --- | --- |
| The horizontal line plots the SOURCE of the money you are going to spend on a given decision | |
| | **Source of The Money** |
| *NOTE: In all cases we are talking about PROFIT portions of money.* | |
| **High Alpha (α)** | Money that you ALREADY have in the bank that you don't have to use for something else. This is the net profit you have ALREADY made from products or services you have ALREADY delivered. |
| **Low Alpha** | The PROFIT portion *(NOT the cost and expense portion)* of money that is <u>currently owed to you</u> for work or products which have already been delivered, but the money isn't in your hands yet (receivables). |
| **Low Beta (β)** | The PROFIT portion of money that <u>will be paid</u> to you when you deliver a product or service which has <u>already</u> been ordered. |
| **High Beta** | The PROFIT portion of money which you plan to make, or project that you are going to make, from the sale of products or services which have not yet been ordered. |
| ***ALL LOAN PROCEEDS ARE HIGH BETA.*** *The money needed to make the loan payments will always come from FUTURE profits.* | |

 **EXTREMELY IMPORTANT! KNOW THIS!**

Revenues have a "cost of goods" (COG) portion and a "profit" portion. Assuming a profit portion of 35%, when your company takes in $100, the profit portion is about $35, <u>NOT $100.</u> The rest is the cost you incur producing and delivering those goods. If you spend the COG portion on something other than the cost of those goods or replacing inventory, you are playing with borrowed money, which is **HIGH BETA.**

## Welcome To Alligator Alley

We've all heard the cute and descriptive saying

> *"It's hard to think about draining the swamp when you're up to your ass in alligators!"*

No experience in life exemplifies that metaphor more accurately than trying to keep your business going when you are being eaten alive by debt and debt-collectors.

The most debilitating part of running a small business is the relentless requirement to feed the cash flow monkey. It's not unusual for a small business to spend its first three or four (or more) years perched precariously on the edge between success and financial chaos. Indeed, the joy of launching one's dream is often overshadowed by the ongoing need for cash.

## Robbing Peter To Pay Paul

One of the reasons that managing waste is so critical in the early years of a business is because "Robbing Peter To Pay Paul" is NOT a business strategy. It is a major distraction from the thing you created your business to do. The more time and energy you spend dodging financial bullets, the less you have to devote to the thing you started your business to do.

But, if you waste your money, you can suddenly – sometimes VERY suddenly – find yourself "swamped" with financial obligations that eat away at your resources and your attention.

Yes, there are times when you have to go out on a financial limb just to keep you doors open. That's part of the deal. But you do huge and unnecessary damage to your chances of success if you climb out on that limb for reasons that your business doesn't need. And when that limb breaks, you are neck deep in "Alligator Alley", aka, **Quadrant III**.

## Alligator Alley

It's not mysterious. If you have to borrow money to pay for something (which is exactly what is happening when you spend BETA money), there will come a point where you gotta have enough cash to pay the bills when they come due. If you get in too deep, life becomes a dark fairy tale. As in battling the wolves at the door.

We've all seen it happen with personal debt. As long as you can get another refinance on the house (more debt), or as long as your salary keeps rising to keep pace with the increasing obligation, you can keep going. But at least you KNOW you are spending borrowed money, even if you do it when you shouldn't.

The problem in a business is that it isn't always clear that you are spending BORROWED money. And no matter how you deal with your personal finances, or how long you have been doing it, you simply can't afford to be slack with your business finances.

> *The ONLY time you should EVER spend borrowed money in your business is if it is necessary for priorities ABOVE THE RISK LINE!*

## Ignorance Doesn't Make It Less Brutal

Just because you don't realize you are spending borrowed money don't expect Alligator Alley to go forgive you. That's why this spending graph is so important.

> **Baby alligators are CUTE, but they'll still rip your arm off when they grow up.**

Anytime you spend money on something your business does not need, you are tossing another baby alligator into the swamp. And the more of those little reptiles you toss in, the less control you have over your business when they grow up. And they WILL grow up!

Once those critters start nipping at your buttocks it's virtually impossible to keep your mind on effectively running your business.

**Robbing Peter and NOT Paying Paul**

One of the biggest casualties of finding yourself in Alligator Alley is your integrity. When you don't have enough money to take care of your obligations, SOMEBODY IS GOING TO GET LEFT OUT.

When that happens, the damage you do to your business reputation and relationships will last even after you figure out how to drain the swamp.

**Your business future depends largely on the promises you MAKE AND KEEP!**

Promises made about money are the most divisive promises made in a business when they are broken. You just don't mess with another dude's money. You don't like it when somebody does that to you and you can't afford to do it to others.

**Glory Days: the other side of the graph**

The place we all want to be on the spending graph is in Quadrant IV. In this case you are spending PROFITS you already have on stuff you just want to buy. Way to go!! Every business owner anywhere definitely wants to get there with you.

Actually, creating the outcome of Glory Days is exactly the preferred outcome of any business venture. All those dreams of freedom and fulfillment come to pass when you get your business to the point where you are doing what you want to do with money you made doing what you want to do. Woo Hoo!!

For the entrepreneur, it doesn't get any better than that.

---

**IMPORTANT NOTE: Spending money like you are in Glory Days when you're really NOT is the quickest route to Alligator Alley. Duh!**

---

## How To Use Merlin's Spending Graph To Make Smart Money Decisions

*If your business is rocking the business cosmos and you have ALL the money you need, this graph could be irrelevant to you. Otherwise, PAY ATTENTION!*

Obviously, the quality of any spending decision depends on how honest you are in assigning priorities and sources of money. This graph is just a tool, like a hammer. If you choose to use your hammer to simply pound your fingers, the hammer won't mind. But used properly, it can help you build some solid stuff.

This graph may not stop you from wasting all of your money, but it will surely provide you with a more solid foundation of information.

> If you BS yourself about the priority, or if you don't know (or care) whether you are really spending profits or other cash, there is NO WAY you can make smart spending decisions. OUCH!

The graph is designed to help in two ways.

1.  It will let you see how you have already spent money. It may be hard to know exactly where the money came from at the time, but by plotting your major spending decisions from the previous year you can get a very clear "picture" of how much financial risk your company is carrying. That knowledge alone can be critical in correcting spending mistakes you might be making.

2.  More important, it lets you see how risky (or necessary) a particular spending decision is before you make it.

Yes, you will still have to gamble on some of your decisions.

Yes, you may very well have to spend Beta money on your business operations.

Your chances of hurting your business increase dramatically the more often you gamble with money you don't have.

It's bad enough when you have to spend borrowed money on essential items (which places your decisions in Quadrant II). It's potential suicide to spend borrowed money on anything else.

**If you are considering spending money where the decision is plotted in Quadrant III, (aka Alligator Alley) DON'T DO IT.**

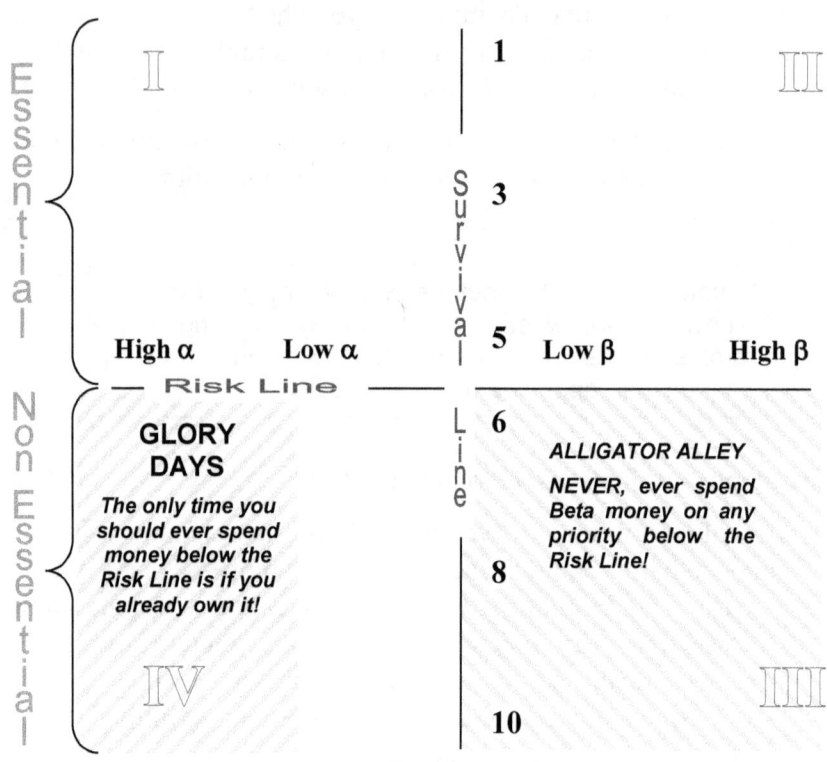

---

*Some Simple Spending Truths*

- *For a typical small business, about 30% of expenditures are Non-Essential (wasted?).*

- *Cutting $1.00 of waste is as good as generating $3.00 of new business (or more!).*

- *You only have to waste $3.00 per day to waste $1,000 per year.*

No matter how well or how bad you think your business is doing, don't let another day pass before you start sniffing out every single nook and cranny where you might be dropping unnecessary money.

## Red Sky In The Morning

There is some old sailor wisdom about the weather that goes, "Red sky in the morning, sailors take warning." The caution being that even though it may be clear and breezy, when the sky is red at sun-up it means that there are things happening in the atmosphere that are going to bring nasty weather. A wise sailor prepares for the inevitable.

Even though everything <u>might</u> look good on the surface, there are some warning signs (red skies) that things are not as perfect as they seem. When one of these signs pop up it is a definite indication that you are playing very close to the edge and it won't take much for you to get in trouble. If you're not already in trouble.

Whatever is happening to your financial picture, you absolutely must know the reality about it. Ignoring the signs, or being overly optimistic about what they mean, is almost certainly going to translate into bad news in the near future.

## Red Sky or Clear Sailing?

If you notice any of these warning signs, it is way past time to start using the Survival Spending graph.

<u>TIGHT CASH FLOW MAY NOT BE A PASSING INCONVENIENCE.</u> While there are a lot of perfectly legitimate reasons why your cash flow may be tight at a given point in time, it is worth noting that tight cash flow means that you are spending more money than you are bringing in. Whenever that happens, it is critical that you do two things.

1. Cut back on spending until the problem reverses itself, not matter how short or long that time frame may be.

2. Don't waste time getting in action!

Find out why your cash flow is tight and make sure you are able to deal with the problem. A tight cash flow may not mean that your business is going south, but if your business is going south one of the first things you will see happening is your monthly cash reserves disappearing. Don't ignore this sign.

PAYROLL PARANOIA. Payroll is a liability that keeps coming up every week or month. It doesn't go away by itself. It should be budgeted like everything else in your business. When you are not able to do that, then you are flirting with big-time problems. One of the brightest Red Sky warnings in business is repeatedly having to sweat it out every payday, hoping that enough money will come in on Friday morning to pay your employees on Friday afternoon.

> *The storm is just over the horizon when you get to the cash-flow state where you have only enough money in the bank to make your net payroll, but you don't have enough money to make the corresponding withholding tax deposits at the same time.*

When this happens you have all the information you will ever need to demonstrate that you have too many employees. You might think you need those employees, *but you can't afford to keep them all.* Make the tough decision as soon as possible. You will hurt your business a lot more by keeping people you

can't afford, than you will by getting rid of some one you think is very good.

MAXED OUT CREDIT LIMITS ARE POISON. It is entirely possible to be doing everything right and still have trouble getting your credit increased with your suppliers. This is one of those areas where small businesses suffer unnecessarily because of restrictive business policies. But whether it is fair, unfair, or just plain stupid, you cannot make money if you don't have products to sell or services to deliver. Having killer sales and no way to ship product is not a whole lot better than having no sales at all.  When you get to the point where you are constantly having to delay shipments because you are backordered from your suppliers, it is time to cut back on sales, or find suppliers who will give you more breathing room.

Maybe this problem is occurring because of rapid growth, or maybe it is occurring because of tardy receivables.  Whatever the reason, when you find yourself up against this particular wall, it is time to seriously evaluate your growth and your spending habits.

HIGHER SALES VOLUMES SHOULD ALWAYS TRANSLATE INTO MORE PROFITS.  One of the problems with us entrepreneurs is we have a tendency to equate large sales volumes with success.  In the frenzy that accompanies growth and impressive revenues, we sometimes forget that our main objective is to make money, and lots of it if possible.

And so we massage our egos by patting our big, strong backs and congratulating ourselves on how big we have become. This *behavior disorder* is enhanced by all those people in the business community who share our paradigm and are equally impressed with our growth. They ask us to speak at seminars and luncheons and they want to interview us for the paper and they always start off by gushing about how breathtaking our revenues are.

Sorry to burst any bubbles, but the thing that really matters is how much profit you have at the end of the day.

> *If you are not increasing profits in some reasonable proportion to your increased revenues, then something is wrong with the core operation.*

As long as the sales curve keeps going up, you will continue to be the center of everyone's attention even if your net profits are anemic  But when that curve levels out, or turns down, then you will have very little time to trim down and get efficient before disaster sets in.

A decline in revenues can happen in a matter of weeks. Cutting wasteful spending takes months.  Revenues WILL decrease at a faster rate than you can cut back your operation.

*And all those people who are so back-slapping happy*
*to have you speak at their lunch won't even be there*
*to buy you lunch when the ka-ka hits the fan.*

Just because one of the above mentioned Red Sky warnings
occurs does not necessarily mean your business is in trouble.  But
is does mean that forces are at work which could very quickly put
your business in trouble if you aren't paying very close attention.

**Even if you think you are doing everything right,**
**don't wait till the last minute to break out the storm gear!**

Since this is a book about business, let's settle on a useful definition of what a business is. One could define a business as

> *An establishment set up to provide a product or service to a customer base by utilization of marketing tactics, incorporating into that product or service the necessary raw materials combined in such a way as to yield a cost effective and profitable end result. .....(yawn).*

For our purposes let's consider another perspective.

> *A business is a series of <u>agreements</u> between you and other parties with whom you will have relations during the course of implementing your business plan.*

It is <u>not</u> inventory (that is products) or money (that is assets or debt) or people (those are employees, vendors, customers, etc.).

It <u>is</u> a *declaration* that a certain series of events <u>will</u> take place. YOU promise to do certain things, such as deliver products, hire people, pay bills, etc. And you count on OTHERS doing the things <u>they</u> promise to do, such as provide you with inventory, pay you for products you deliver, come to work on time, etc.

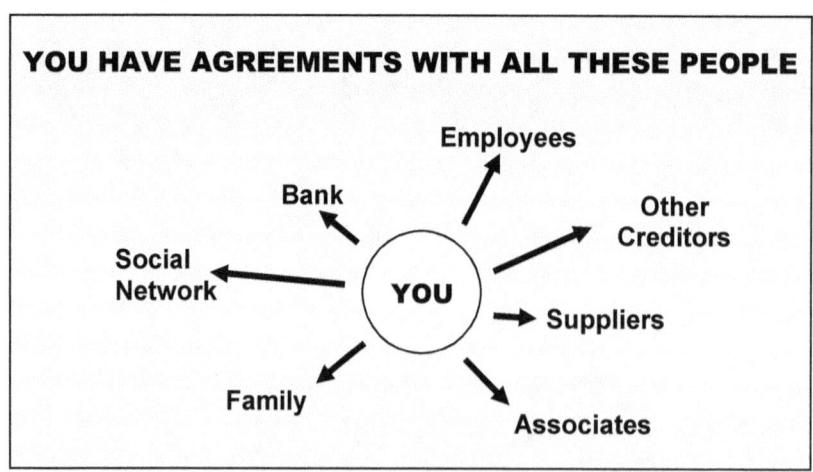

**YOU HAVE AGREEMENTS WITH ALL THESE PEOPLE**

Employees

Bank

Other Creditors

Social Network

YOU

Suppliers

Family

Associates

The very documents you created to establish your business are *agreements* between you and the municipality in which you do business. Your business checking account is an *agreement* between you and the bank.

## Agreements And Power

Understanding the nature of *agreements* requires understanding the nature POWER – specifically, the power to make and keep those agreements. Agreeing to do something you have no power to do is a fast-track to destroying your credibility.

As you might expect, there are different types of power and different sources of it. The diagram below illustrates these sources of power. (*A detailed description of the Sources of Power can be found in the Appendix at the end of this book.*)

### Sources of Power in Business

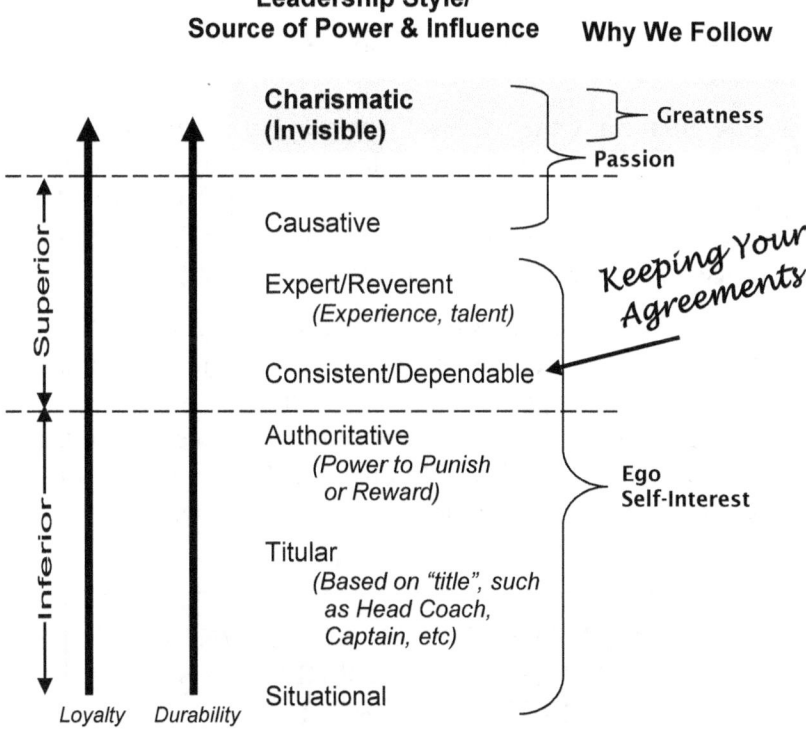

There are two things to notice in the previous diagram.

1.  The degree of power and influence a person has increases as you go up the chart. "Charismatic" power is way more effective and durable than "Titular" power.

2.  The *loyalty* people generate is directly related to the actual source of the power.

While it may seem that these sources of power are only available to certain people in certain situations, the fact is, they are available to ANYONE. In fact, you are constantly operating inside these powers whether you realize it or not.

**Every Relationship You Have In Your Business Is Defined By This Power Graph.**

Either you have the power, or the other person has it. But it is there, and it is at work in its unique way. And it dramatically influences the agreements you make every day.

**The Relationship Between Power and Agreements**

Two criteria must exist if a person is going to enter into any agreement.

**1. She must have the necessary <u>power</u> (authority) to enter into an agreement in the first place.** For example, a sales person may have the power to set a price, or promise a delivery date, but she probably does NOT have the power to promise to reorganize the company's marketing team.

**2. She must be willing <u>and able</u> (have enough power) to deliver the agreement as promised.** One of the most telling Red Sky Warnings you will ever get with regards to an agreement is when someone says "We'll do something, even if it's not right!" , or "We'll figure something out." Clearly, this person does not have the power to deliver on the agreement.

> **NEVER ENTER INTO AN AGREEMENT IF YOU AND THE OTHER PARTY CAN'T SPECIFY THE PROMISE.**

In the absence of those two criteria, <u>there simply cannot be a true agreement</u>. Even if everything is well-intentioned, somebody's expectations will not be met. That is ALWAYS a precursor to THAT person being really ticked off.

If you are making an agreement with someone, you probably assume that <u>both</u> of those criteria are in place. But are they? It's definitely worth it to take the time to ensure that BOTH of these criteria are solidly in place with all of your agreements.

**Another Aspect of The Relationship Between Power And Agreements. And It's More Important.**

The way you handle agreements is a critical part of developing power to begin with. While an entry-level employee may have limited power *overall*, that employee can exercise many of these kinds of power at whatever level they are.

For example, a shipping clerk probably will only have limited opportunities to be a charismatic visionary for their company. But, with regard to the various responsibilities of a shipping clerk, that employee can absolutely drive their own reputation and influence by understanding and embracing the traits of these power levels.

As a business owner, you will constantly reinforce or sabotage your reputation and business relationships every time you make an agreement, and every time you deliver some result from that agreement.

---

**Basic Rules Of Agreements:**

1. Only make agreements you have the power to make.

2. Do whatever it takes to fulfill every agreement you make.

---

When you follow these Basic Rules, you will *consistently and dependably* do the things you agree to do. Referring back to the Power Diagram, notice that "Being Consistent and Dependable" is one of the SUPERIOR sources of power and influence. No matter who you deal with, or what your position is inside a business, mastering Consistent Power is a huge plus for your reputation.

This shouldn't be surprising. Whether in business or your personal life, you probably prefer to deal with people that are authentic and you know what to expect from them. Everyone else does too. When you deliver the agreements you say you will, no matter how large or small, you create a space of certainty and confidence among your associates.

This confidence extends in all directions - inside your business, with your customers and with your business associates. What's not to love about THAT? In a small business that is a priceless asset.

Even the most limited kinds of power can be very effective tools in developing a reputation. In fact, how you manage the power you have WILL define your reputation in and out of your business. And it WILL have a dramatic effect on your success.

**Agreements Are Promises**

When you make an agreement with another party, regardless of the specifics, you *promise* to do something. Usually the other party promises to do something of similar value, and so a mutual benefit results.

Naturally, you expect the other party to deliver on their promise, and unless there have been conditions built into the agreement,

**you don't want <u>excuses</u>, you want <u>the benefit</u>!**

On the flip side, you are obliged to deliver on your promise and provide the benefit to your counterpart as well.

**Re-Introducing HAIRBALLS**

*Remember the hairball distinction from the beginning of this book (page 7)? If not, GO BACK AND READ IT NOW!*

You will recall that no single agreement you make is necessarily a big deal. But the collection of them all together is a force to be reckoned with. It includes every agreement you made and every result or interpretation that resulted. Good or bad, regardless of the reasons (excuses), it becomes your REPUTATION.

## What happens in life when someone doesn't deliver on a promise to YOU?

No need to expand on the nasty implications, suffice it to say that a barrier is created in the relationship between you and the other party. If enough barriers are created, or if they are huge enough, the relationship between the parties crumbles. Worse, it can even become *adversarial*.

Your very existence as a business owner depends on the quality of the agreements you make, and the quality of the people with whom you make them. Squandering your good will and integrity is every bit as deadly as squandering your cash.

And speaking of cash, if you are dealing with an agreement that has to do with money (and most of them do in a business), the blowback from not fulfilling the promised result is exponentially more negative, the resentments are longer lasting and the resulting lack of confidence is more deeply entrenched.

## Are There Some Agreements You Can Get Away With Not Keeping?

Don't even go there. If you make it, don't break it! Do everything you can to keep your agreements.

> *You don't want to be known as "That guy who ... (doesn't keep their word, doesn't get it done, doesn't deliver, etc.)"*

## Obsessing About Your Agreements Can Drive You Crazy. Or It Can Be Really Smart.

Either way, if you are ready to elevate how seriously you are in fulfilling your agreements, you'll need to elevate how serious you are about making them in the first place. You have to be willing to be responsible for the fulfillment of <u>every</u> agreement you make.

> **REMEMBER The Basic Rules Of Agreements:**
>
> 1. Only make agreements you have the power to make.
>
> 2. Do whatever it takes to fulfill every agreement you make.

## If You Break It, CLEAN IT UP!

In spite of your best efforts, you will break agreements. It just goes with the turf. When that happens you must manage the negative consequences quickly and with honor.

You may not be able to completely restore the benefit of the original agreement, but you can at least apologize for, and take responsibility for, the broken promise. If there is a way to compensate your counterpart (a free product, complimentary services, discounts, etc), you can go along way toward restoring or maintaining your reputation by providing them.

This is not the time to make excuses! However, you have every right to make your case. Just remember. Your counterpart will either be left with the benefit you promised or the story you give about why you broke your promise.

Choose wisely.

## The Anatomy Of An Agreement

An agreement consists of three parts:

1. The proposal

2. The acceptance of the proposal (promise) and,

3. The fulfillment (delivering the benefit).

A proposal without a promise is simply on offer and requires no action. An agreement is not being negotiated until one of the parties *promises* to deliver some benefit. Equally clearly, if you accept the proposal, you are obligated to deliver the benefit.

In order for a reliable agreement to take place, there must be a conscious recognition that all parties to the agreement will benefit from it in some way. Unfortunately, the specific benefits are not always articulated beforehand. It's worth pointing out, the less reliable the benefits, the less reliable the agreement.

## The Making Of An Agreement

One party presents a PROPOSAL and the other party ACCEPTS OR DECLINES the proposal.

**Proposal  + Acceptance of Proposal = Agreement**

AND

**Agreement + Delivery on the Agreement = Fulfilled Agreement**

Not all promises involve an agreement, but all agreements involve at least one promise. And that promise is a fundamental part of who you are and what your business is all about. In fact, you will become known by the promises you <u>make</u>.

---

*NEVER FORGET!*

*Your friends, customers, employees and vendors will define <u>who you are</u> by how <u>dependable you are</u> at delivering on your <u>promises</u>.*

---

## No Place For Excuses

Let's look at the Agreement Formula again.

**Proposal  + Acceptance of Proposal = Agreement**

AND

**Agreement + Delivery on the Agreement = Fulfilled Agreement**

Do you see anything in there about *excuses*? Nope. The formula does not allow a place for excuses. What would it look like if it did?

**Agreement +** 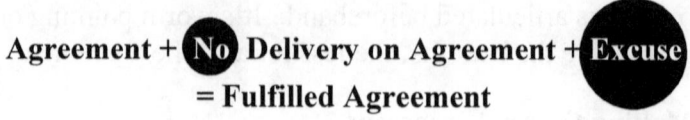 **No Delivery on Agreement + Excuse**
**= Fulfilled Agreement**

Hmmmm. Doesn't seem quite the same.

**EXAMPLE: A late employee**

The agreement is: You pay your employee money and that person starts work at 8:00.

**$$$$ + Employee starts work at 8:00 = Fulfilled Agreement**

As long as you pay the money, and as long as the employee starts work at 8:00, everyone is doing their part and the agreement is fulfilled.

Now, let's look at the "excuse" version.

**$$$$ + Employee doesn't start work at 8:00 <u>but has a really good excuse</u>**
**= Fulfilled Agreement**

Well, that may work for the person being late, but clearly it doesn't work for you. After all,

## "Employee starts work at 8:00"

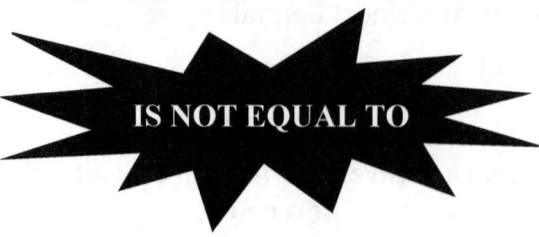

IS NOT EQUAL TO

## "Employee <u>doesn't</u> start work at 8:00, but has a really good excuse."

We can NEVER use an excuse in place of a delivery on a promise, at least not if we expect people to have confidence in us.

> *The expectation that an agreement will be fulfilled is one of the most powerful forces that you can use in gaining the support and confidence of your employees, customers and vendors.*

**The Implied Agreement** *(aka "What the Heck Just Happened?")*

Quite often, the critical step of ACCEPTING the proposal is *implied* rather than articulated. Such an arrangement happens when there is a general understanding, but not specifics. Unfortunately for one of the parties, even though one side of the agreement is implied rather than articulated, that side of the agreement must still be honored.

For example, if your neighbor borrows your garden hose to wash his car, and you don't say anything about it, it is "implied" that you are okay with that arrangement. If he does it more than once, and you never say anything, you reinforce the "agreement".

Likewise, suppose you agree to give a co-worker a ride to work assuming she is going to pitch in for gas. But she doesn't offer and you still give her a ride each day. It is *implied* that you are in agreement with that arrangement.

Such an agreement process can be disastrous for a small business in so many ways. Going back to our example of the late employee, if you tolerate the late arrival over time, you have replaced the original agreement with an *implied* agreement that says you agree to accepting the excuses.

Other things that often get tolerated and thus become implied agreements that you must honor:

- Customers who pay later than your terms, but you still continue to ship products;
- Suppliers or vendors who do not meet delivery dates, but you still do business with them;
- Employees that deliver sub-standard customer service, but you don't discipline or correct them;

- Customers that add on features or services after the sale and you don't adjust the bill to cover the increases;

There are a lot of justifications for continuing to tolerate these *implied*, but unacceptable, agreements. You may want to keep a customer happy, or you may think you need to keep a particular vendor, or you may not have the time to manage a particular employee.

> ***Whatever your justifications, implied agreements will sabotage your best efforts, over and over and over.***

Regardless of the inconvenience or upset you may have to endure, you are ALWAYS better off by not allowing implied agreements to stay in place.

## The Course Of Dealing

Sometimes in business dealings there are disputes that result in legal actions. One of the most prevalent is some version of a "Breach of Contract". Basically, this is a legal accusation that someone didn't keep their side of an agreement. In most cases, the basis of the complaint is some form of "contract" between the parties, usually one that is written.

Most people would assume that if there is a written contract, and one party doesn't honor their side, this is a clear violation and a slam dunk.

## Not So Fast.

In a legal setting, the way you actually conduct business (the actual "course" of your "dealings" with the other party) will often out-weigh the original contract.

For example, suppose you have a contract that says you will receive delivery of widgets by the 15th of each month. But you routinely don't get your widgets until the 20th. Maybe this doesn't work for you, but for whatever reason, you put up with the late deliveries for several months. Until you can't stand it anymore.

Then you punish the supplier by deducting penalties for late delivery when you pay your bill. Your justification for changing *your* part of the agreement is that the other party isn't keeping *their* part. One thing leads to another until you find yourself in court.

Your supplier could <u>legally</u> make a case that, regardless of the written contract, you had been *dealing* with the existing process with no complaint just fine for several months. And so the supplier had every right to expect you to continue on the same *course* in the future.

The point here is not to have a legal conversation. It is to illustrate that:

> *It is reasonable for people to expect you to continue to operate the way you are operating, even if it is in violation of a previous agreement.*

When you notice an implied agreement in place you must acknowledge it quickly. You may decide to keep it in place, or you may decide to end it and re-instate the original agreement. But DO NOT ignore the "course of your dealings" in the matter. If you do, you are giving your consent to the implied agreement, and your counterpart could rightly assume you are willing to accept the implied agreement.

**Agreements Regarding Money**

Not keeping your agreements will ALWAYS cause you problems. And not keeping your agreements with regard to money matters is like spraying gas on a match.

Unless you are operating in a barter economy, your business simply cannot survive without cash flow, both in and out. ANY constraint on that cash flow, such as credit restrictions or late paying customers, makes an already difficult job almost impossible.

*Messing around with somebody else's money is a risky and volatile world to travel in. People tend to take it really personal. And if by you failing to keep <u>your</u> agreements, you cause them to not keep <u>their</u> agreements, you've probably made an enemy for life.*

In the world of business, money is the ultimate prize. Being trusted about money matters is therefore an extraordinary asset. But if people don't trust you with money matters, they will only do business with you if they have no other options. Talk about constricting your cash flow!

## You Always Get What You Reward

If you reward people for paying you late, they will keep doing it. Remember, cash "flow" is IN and OUT. The "in" part must happen if <u>you</u> are going to keep <u>your</u> agreements. When you tolerate late pays, you are rewarding people for making your job so much harder. Why would you do that?

> **Continuing to do business with customers who don't keep their money agreements is like paying somebody else's car payment while you have to ride the bus. (#dumb).**

## If You Need An Excuse, Any One Will Do!

A few years back a high school PTA checked with the teachers to find out the most common excuses students used when not turning in homework. The idea was to do a humorous article for the last newsletter of the year. The results were not particularly surprising. You may have even used a few of them yourself.

## Some Things Never Change

If somebody is using one of these excuses on you, that is a huge red flag regarding the integrity of that person or business. If you continue to do business with them, you <u>will</u> get burned at some point.

And of course, if YOU are using any of these excuses, you are obviously NOT using your Spending Graph, and you are NOT keeping your money agreements. Double Deadly. Deadly. Deadly.

**TOP 5 LATE HOMEWORK EXCUSES AND THEIR MODERN DAY VERSIONS.**

*They were BS then. They're BS now.*

| Late Homework Excuse | | Late Pay Excuse |
|---|---|---|
| "What homework?" | | "Gee, we never got that invoice. Can you resend it?" |
| "I didn't understand the assignment." | | "We had some question about that invoice." |
| Some version of "The dog ate it." | | Some version of "I thought we mailed that payment" or "The check's in the mail" |
| "I was sick" <br> • my baby brother was sick, <br> • my mom was sick <br> • …. blah, blah, blah)" | | "I'm sorry, I (we) have been <br> • Sick <br> • Recovering from a fire <br> • A computer crash <br> • … (blah, blah, blah) |

## Agreement Creep

Over time, almost any agreement will change to accommodate routine circumstances. Whether it is employees starting on time, suppliers delivering products or customers paying their bills, it's not unusual for the parties to adapt to circumstances in order to accommodate each other.

This is may not be a problem. Being flexible can be one of the advantages of operating a small business, as opposed to being stuck in the rigid structure of an impersonal corporate process.

But BEWARE! Making routine accommodations over time can result in a whole new agreement being morphed into place without you even noticing it. This can completely catch you off guard because it happens slowly over weeks or months. It *creeps* into place, one little accommodation at a time.

Agreement Creep is the NORMAL process of maintaining agreements over time. It is the natural way people work together. It does not necessarily mean that one party is trying to take advantage of the other. But it can result in one party being disadvantaged, even if it is unintentional.

You must stay vigilant to ensure that your agreements maintain their original intention. And you must be honorable enough to address Agreement Creep even when it benefits your position more than your counterpart.

> *Our society could not exist without agreements*

### And Neither Can Your Business!

Spend the time and mental effort to fully understand your agreements. And do whatever you can to honor those that you make. It is not a "one-time" thing. It is an ongoing process. Doing it right will provide your business with an essential, powerful tool and a competitive edge. Doing it wrong will result in one of the most deadly Self-Inflicted wounds your business can suffer.

## The Double-Edged Sword

Employees can be your biggest asset. They can also be the most frustrating and detrimental part of operating your business. Particularly if you are in the 95%. It is absolutely imperative that you manage this area of your business with consistency and fairness at all times.

More than products, location, and profits, employees dictate the flow of your business at every level. Good ones can propel you to extraordinary heights. Bad ones can sabotage everything you do.

One reason is because a small business has so few employees compared to large companies. According to the U.S. Labor statistics, "small business" generally means fewer than 500 employees and less than $7 million in annual receipts.

More relevant to you is that 95% of all U.S businesses employee less than 10 employees, and generate less than $250,000 in annual receipts. And that includes doctor's practices and lawyer's legal offices.

So, if you are part of the 95% of business owners who fit that category, one bad employee represents at least 10% of your work force. Now THAT can be a scary thought!

## And You're Not Alone

A recent study of small business owners showed that, on average, almost half of all business owners were as *dissatisfied* with their staffs as they were satisfied with them. On average, owners were:

- Very pleased and satisfied          22%
- Reasonably satisfied                31%
- Neither satisfied or dissatisfied   26%
- Very dissatisfied                   19%

> *Almost 50% of business owners are unimpressed or outright dissatisfied with their current staff of employees.*

## Most Small Business Owners Are Entrepreneurs, NOT Managers

It's often been said of small businesses that the person who starts the business is often NOT the best person to run the business. Unless you have formal training in business management, you'd pretty much expect that to be the case. Entrepreneurs are dreamers and visionaries and risk-takers. The adventurous kind of thinking it takes to launch a business in the first place comes from a different skill set than the organized objective kind of thinking it takes to keep an organization running smoothly.

If we last long enough, we'll learn how to balance those two worlds. It is one of the challenges of being a small business owner, perhaps the only one that really matters. Being qualified to start a business DOES NOT mean we are qualified to run it. Alas, we have no choice but to learn if we are going to succeed.

Even though we may not be qualified to manage a business, we can really improve our chances of success if we make sure that the people we hire are qualified to do their job.

## Which Means We Have To Know What That Job Is

The first thing to keep in your mind when hiring an employee is:

### The firing process begins the day the person is hired.

When you add an employee to your business you also add

- Payroll taxes
- Benefits of some sort
- Investments in time and money to train the employee
- Physical changes to the work environment to accommodate the new employee
- Some change in the dynamics of how your company operates on a day to day basis

When we hire a person, we expect all of those things to happen and we expect (hope?) that the overall result of will be a positive one for your business.

But that positive result doesn't happen automatically. In fact, based on the numbers shown earlier, it doesn't happen at all 50% of the time. If you are going to ensure that your hiring decisions are positive contributions to your business you must know what you are hiring someone to do.

## Hiring The Right Person Isn't Always An Easy Thing To Do

But it is essential that we get as good a work force as we can, given our time and money. That means we have to be flexible in our hiring. There is a lot of job overlap in small businesses because there are fewer people to do everything that needs to be done.

Therefore, we <u>must</u> focus our hiring attention on providing the CORE competencies we need, even if the overall job must also include other accountabilities. Regardless of the size of your business, there are certain <u>areas of operation</u> in your business that you must manage.

To the degree possible, you should hire people who are qualified and <u>well-suited for these areas</u>. If you're lucky, you will find people who can handle multiple areas. Otherwise, <u>you</u> will have to pick up the slack.

**Do yourself a huge favor. Hire the skills you need, not just the people you like.**

## The General Areas Of Any Business Operation

The following is not an exhaustive description. It's more like an invitation to consider the diversity of the picture you are dealing with.

- Operations – everything involved in acquiring your product, delivering it to the customers and getting paid for it. Also includes all aspects of personnel functions, including payroll.

- Product research/development – everything involved in determining <u>what</u> you are going to sell, and matching up products you sell with customer demographics. Whatever your product or service, you must have the expertise needed to deliver that service or product.

- Physical Plant – Your physical environment includes everything from staples and printer paper, to the vehicles you use to deliver your product or service, technology you use. Making sure you have a secure, efficient operating space is important. Keeping the light bulbs replaced and emptying the trash is also important.

- Sales – in many cases you'll see "Sales" and "Marketing" as a single item – "Sales & Marketing". But in a small business, these two areas need to be <u>intentionally split</u> and thought about in different ways. "Sales" is all of the activities and expenses <u>directly</u> related to completing a financial transaction with your customer. If we consider a grocery store, "Sales" happens when a person goes to the register and pays for their food.

- Marketing – except for activities that allow you to create an online presence, if you are part of the 95%, you might want to consider ignoring this category for the first 6 - 12 months of your business life. The likelihood that you will waste massive amounts of money on activities that make absolutely no difference is <u>far more dangerous</u> to a young business than possibly missing out on creating new customers. If you do decide to enter this enchanted forest, this area includes all of your advertising, promotions, networking and branding.

> ***Even if you are a one-person operation you STILL have to manage the essential tasks in all of these areas.***

When you hire people, always keep that in mind! If you hire unnecessary or unqualified people, you create enormous obstacles for yourself.

Use the hiring process as a tool to help you accomplish your dreams. That's why you started this whole thing, right? Don't blow your chances by treating the hiring process like you are choosing what color to paint your office.

**The Hiring Process 101**

Yes, it's easier said than done. Get over it. This is what you must learn to do and the sooner the better.

Not surprisingly, the entrepreneur is not always a good job interviewer. In many cases, the person who starts their own business has never had to even manage people, much less hire someone.

Be prepared to make mistakes when you hire. In large companies, the hiring process can involve a dozen people and take several months for mid-level positions, and even more for key positions. You can't go that far. But you can absolutely elevate the intentionality and leadership you exhibit during the hiring process.

You may feel that you don't have to bother with this level of commitment because you are too small.

DEADLY mistake.

The smaller your business, the <u>more critical</u> each individual hire is.

> **If you are in the 95%, almost every position you fill will be a <u>key</u> position. Hire accordingly.**

**Have Understandable Job Descriptions.**

Make a *conscious* decision about what tasks you <u>must</u> have and which ones you are going to let go. Creating good, clear job descriptions helps <u>you</u> every bit as much as it helps your employee. Once you create that job description, stick to it.

Don't hire someone with a Job Description of "Answer The Phones" and then add in the job of "Clean The Restrooms". When circumstances require you to modify a job, do what you have to do. But include the employee in the process as much as possible.

One of the biggest sources of dissatisfaction from the employee's perspective is being treated like tools or pieces of furniture.

When your message (even if you don't say it) is something like

*"You'll do anything I say because you work for me",*

employees begin to feel trapped or taken advantage of. You will undermine best intentions of your employees by keeping them guessing about what their job actually is.

> *The relationship with your employees as it pertains to expectations about what their job includes is THE area in your business where you are most likely to abuse "Authoritative Power".*

You will create resentment and unrest when you add requirements to existing jobs without a reasonable explanation.

> Question: Why would you want to create fear, resentment and unrest?
>
> Answer: YOU WOULDN'T!

So don't.

## Your Employees: A Critical Asset That You Have The Most Control Over.

Don't sabotage that advantage. As the boss, you might be able to force your employees to submit to your demands, but you will never get their best effort if they feel like they are being used. You NEED their best effort!

## Have Specific Hiring Criteria.

Once you create Job Descriptions that reflect what you need, do the mental work necessary to understand what skills that job requires. If you need bookkeeping, don't hire someone whose main *skill* is fixing car engines.

*One of the <u>worst hiring mistakes</u> you can make is to hire someone who does <u>not</u> have the skills for a particular job because they're cheap, or because you think you can control the person, such as a friend or family member.*

**If You Can't Say What Skills A Person Must Have, How Can You Possibly Know If They Are Doing A Good Job At Using Their Skills?**

A big-time self-inflicted wound is to not have a clear picture of whether or not your employees are doing what you need to be done. You can't know that unless you know what the job requires. (#duh)

Know everything you can about what skills the job requires. Spell it out for <u>yourself</u>. If you need meticulous attention to numbers, you don't want to make the mistake of hiring someone whose strength is skinning rabbits.

**Once You Have Specific Skills To Evaluate, EVALUATE.**

Nobody likes the process of evaluating employees. But you need a way to know whether or not your staff is doing their jobs well. In a small business you don't necessarily have to create a detailed Employee Review structure. But you DO need to know if you are getting what you need. Use that criteria on a regular basis to determine if that is happening.

Despite the warnings, the unfortunate reality is that you will likely put up with sub-standard performance much longer than you should. That is also human nature. But when the time comes where you are no longer going to tolerate such, you need to have solid reasons for taking action.

Ironically, you won't think it's important to set up this criteria until you have a problem with an employee, and that's too late. Bite the bullet and do it now.

**The Best Way To Improve Performance From Employees: Let Them Know What Is Expected Of Them.**

People hate not knowing what their job is, and they REALLY

hate not knowing whether or not they are doing it right. Remember, *the firing process begins the day the person is hired.*

The very criteria you need to evaluate and compensate your good employees is the information you will need to discipline or terminate problem employees.

## You Will ALWAYS Get What You Reward

Of all the agreements you make in your business, the ones you make with your employees are perhaps the most critical. Not just the *declared* agreements you make during the hiring process, but the *implied* agreements that evolve over time.

Rewarding a behavior or result doesn't always require that you openly declare your approval for *positive* outcomes, it often only requires that you do nothing to correct *negative* outcomes.

On the other hand, openly demonstrating your approval for desired outcomes communicates a valuable message. Remember, employees are primarily interested in job security and fairness. Your authentic and consistent approval fulfills both of those needs in a big way.

## Money Isn't Everything, But It Matters To Both Parties

The pay scale you set up when you hire someone will be a monkey that needs to be fed <u>forever</u>. Pay every penny you can afford for the <u>right</u> skills, and NOT A PENNY MORE

- Have a pay scale set up before you hire
- Don't give raises based solely on need
- Don't give raises based on other employee's wages
- Don't give advances against future payroll

## Basic Characteristics of Any Employee

Anyone you hire is going to have a personal history and pattern of experience that probably has little to do with your business. They may have skills you need, but they are not in the game for the same reasons you are.

Remember, employees are motivated by <u>security</u> and <u>fairness</u>.

Just because <u>you</u> have are prepared to hock your future for your vision of a "better mousetrap", don't expect people who work for you to appreciate or understand your dream.

You can certainly require competence and professional performance from your employees, but you have very little chance of getting your employees to demonstrate the same level of commitment that <u>you</u> put into the company. And you have NO right to expect it either.

**You especially DO NOT have the right to expect your employees to take personal hits (long hours, irregular pay, poor working conditions, etc.) just because you do.**

### Set High Standards. Keep It Real.

There is a limit to what you can expect from people who work for you. This limit is not a mysterious barrier. Just realize that if your workers had your independence and desire for a challenge, they would be your *competitors*.

An employee is a person who will leave your company one day. You just don't know when or under what circumstances. In hard economic times, people will tolerate a lot of stuff they don't like, but that is purely *Situational*.

Over the long haul, employee's loyalty to you is directly related to their sense of job security and how fairly they think they are being treated. Everything else is secondary. Don't lose sight of that brutal reality.

### Types Of Employees

You have your reasons for hiring people, and they have their reasons for coming to work for you. Since you are so dependant on them to make your business succeed, it's a good idea to understand <u>their</u> reality.

One of the most prevalent mistakes small business owner make in hiring and managing employees is to assume that people you hire should share your level of commitment to your business. That assumption will lead you to upset and disappointment. Worse still from the employee perspective, it could cause you to unfairly judge the people who work for you. Bad energy!

## People Have Different Levels Of "Buy In" When They Take A Job.

If you are hiring a store manager, you want someone who will go beyond the minimum and invest themselves in your business. But if you are hiring a receivables clerk, or a hot dog vendor, you shouldn't expect that person to have the same sense of urgency about your business.

All employees will have some level of "buy-in" for your business. Obviously, you want the store manager to "Buy In" at a higher level than the receivables clerk might. But just because a person doesn't give you a high level of buy-in <u>does not mean</u> they are not a valuable employee. Know the difference.

## Four Levels Of Buy-In Of Your Business Mission

- <u>Not particularly interested in your mission</u>. These folks need a job – and pretty much anything will do. Or they need a better job than the one they had, some kind of upgrade from their previous job (more money, better hours, closer to home, benefits, etc.). For these guys, how much they make and what kind of work environment they experience is the main motivator. Maybe the only motivator.

- <u>Interested in your mission.</u> They might even be impressed by it, but they are not committed enough to sacrifice for you. As long as you keep your promises to them, they will do a good job for you and will take pride in the results they produce. They are building something, maybe even with your business, so it matters to them how well they do. But don't expect this group to stick around when things get really tough. And don't expect them to be sympathetic

  if you experience personal hardship. They are acutely aware of <u>their own needs</u> for money and stability. If you can't provide that, they will take their skills elsewhere at the first opportunity.

- Supports your mission. These guys like your philosophy and they like their job.  More importantly, they are willing to put some skin in the game. That doesn't necessarily mean they are "in it for the long haul come hell or high water".  But it does mean that they will take the job seriously and will strive to support your way of doing things.

- Willing to be responsible for your mission. This is who you want managing your store.  While favoritism is not generally a good policy, these are the people who are going to help you multiply your efforts and you should show your appreciation.  These employees are actually invested in your vision.  Treat them well and allow them to contribute.

---

**BIG MISTAKE**

**Thinking that the only good employee is one who is willing to be responsible for your vision.**

---

### The Perfect Employee

Several years ago, Dr. Sherry Kuckenbecher, a Sports Psychologist at Loyola-Marymount University, conducted an exhaustive survey of coaches at all levels to define "scientifically" what actually constituted the "Traits of a Winner". The paper she wrote by the same name outlined the process she used, and identified 5 Traits that large majorities of coaches from youth sports to the Olympics said were the key to being a winner.

---

**The Traits Of A Winner**
*(Dr. Shari Kuchenbecker, Loyola Marymount University August 1999)*

| | |
|---|---|
| *Loves the Game* | *Positive Attitude* |
| *Coachable* | *Self-motivated* |
| *Team Player* | *Strives to Improve* |

---

The most striking revelation of her research was the disconnect between these winning traits and the traits that typically drive recruiting (aka "hiring"). Her research revealed that the most prevalent *recruiting* criteria were talent, strength, physical dominance, and natural skills.

But those traits were actually at the <u>bottom</u> of the list of traits that coaches deemed were essential in the making of a winner. In other words, coaches selected players with strength, skill and physical dominance (i.e., specific skills), but they did NOT recruit for those traits of being a winner.

As a business owner, you are obviously hiring for a particular skill set. And if you have vast resources and can recruit (i.e., hire) the absolute best in the field, perhaps you don't need to worry so much about these traits.

But, if you are part of the 95%, you probably can't shell out top dollar for your employees. Still, you can exponentially increase the value of your "recruits" by looking for the "Traits Of A Winner" in the process. In fact, it may be the edge you are looking for. It's an asset that you have available to you. Take advantage of it.

And, by the way. Similar research has shown repeatedly that the very teams that win games they should lose ("under dogs", "giant killers", "spoilers", etc.), are the teams that have high levels of "winning traits".

> **You can compensate for not being able to hire proven superstars by hiring "winners" and then helping them become superstars.**

### Coherence Starts With Your Employees.

If you didn't read about the Coherence Factor earlier in the book (page 8), you should do it now. This conversation will make a lot more sense if you know what we're talking about.

How well you apply the Coherence Factor to your hiring will be one of the few chances you have to stack the deck in your favor. By bringing that environment of "coherence" right from the beginning you enhance the value of the every skill you bring into your company.

You want your company to run as close to "smoothly" as it can. Coherence provides that. When you create coherence, you have people operating on the same page right from the beginning.

Conversely, randomly hired people, with no consideration for the coherence of the business, *interrupt* the flow of energy, even to the point of creating chaos. You've seen examples of how one person can cause dissension in a group. That is a prime example of "incoherence". Given the small number of employees in a small business, one bad apple <u>can indeed</u> spoil the whole bunch.

***Incoherence will be more decisive in limiting what your business can accomplish than any other set of circumstances you will encounter!***

To the degree you can promote coherence with your hiring process, you should absolutely do that. You will dramatically improve your chances of success and the pace at which it arrives.

## Hiring "Down"

This is when you hire someone for a job that is below their previous work and earnings history. Sometimes a person will be completely willing to give up both more money and more autonomy for less stress and responsibility. But sometimes (more often) this person is taking the best job they can get, even if it's not what they really want.

The Up-Side:

- You may not have to provide as much training or supervision

- You often get additional skills that you wouldn't get otherwise

The Down-Side:

- This is probably a "temp" situation. This employee will always be trying to get back to where they were, even if the desire to do so is subconscious. Unless you are able to accommodate their desire to get back to the job level they previously had, they'll always be looking.

- This employee may chafe under the closer supervision that comes with the job, which can result in resentment and resistance to managerial input.

## Don't Assume the Next Level *(The Michael Jordan Effect)*

We all know that Michael Jordan was the greatest basketball player of his time. But when he took over *managing* a team, he was a disaster.

A good salesman doesn't necessarily make a good sales *manager*. The same can be said for almost any situation where there are added responsibilities, *especially* if any of those responsibilities involve managing people in a new job.

Examples:

| **Promoting** | **To** |
|---|---|
| Sales Person | Sales Manager |
| Mechanic | Service Manager |
| Cook | Restaurant Manager |

Of course you will want to reward people who do a good job for you. And you will want to expand areas of responsibility to those who know how to get things done. Look for that ability. But don't assume it's there!

Promoting someone who isn't qualified doesn't do them any favors. And it often doesn't work very well for the people they manage. If you promote someone who doesn't have the skill set and you know it, it's YOUR job to make sure they get the training they need

It's a lot harder to demote someone, or fire them, than it is to not promote (or hire) them in the first place.

This applies whether you are hiring a new employee or promoting one you've already got.

### NEVER REWARD SOMEONE FOR PERSONAL REASONS BY PROMOTING THEM!

**Other circumstances that often become problems you can't easily get rid of are:**

- Hiring family or close friends
- Hiring someone because they will work for less than the going rate,
- Hiring someone who is "doing you a favor"

## Don't Hire People You Don't Need

As important as that one point is, there are other very good reasons why you should strive to keep your workforce lean.

- There is no single expenditure you can make that will hurt your cash position more than having unnecessary people around, or paying more than you can afford.

- Unnecessary employees will be a major distraction to everyone involved. And don't fool yourself into thinking that you need these people when it is slow so you can train them for when "things pick up." Historically, the odds are that things will pick up much more slowly than you predict. In the mean time, the money and time you invest goes on.

- A really good way to determine if you have too many employees is this:

  *Are able to make the entire payroll every time (including withholdings, unemployment taxes, etc.), or do you routinely have only enough money to pay the net payroll?*

This isn't necessarily deadly if it only happens occasionally, But it should always be a red flag. If it happens regularly and you *don't* have the resources to cover it, you need to downsize immediately.

Sometimes the small business mind-set equates numbers of employees with some measure of success. This is certainly understandable, but this perception actually belongs in one of the "BS" categories we discussed in Chapter 1.

Getting rid of someone you think might be good "down the road" will hurt you a lot less than keeping someone you don't need or can't afford.

## Creative Compensation

Don't try to compete with everybody else on dollars alone. There are a lot of ways you can compensate employees for great performance, longevity or special skills. And never forget the old saying "Familiarity breeds contempt".

Any time you give an employee a raise, it is just a matter of time before "Hey, thanks for the raise" morphs into, "What have you done for me this week?" If your response to that dialog is always to give more money, you create an upward spiral of financial commitment that stresses your cash flow and doesn't necessarily improve your status with your employees.

- Try giving something other than money. Memorable experiences often outweigh more money. Concert tickets, a gift certificate for a great restaurant, a weekend get-away, even a TV can make a way bigger positive impression. Also consider this – a $500 "gift" is the same amount of money as a 20 cents per hour raise. How far do you think that .20/hr will go in making you look like a great boss? But a TV?

- Provide tools or technology that support the job. Obvious examples are a company car, a computer or a cell phone. A good idea if you can do it, but those can get pricey and you don't always have control over how they get used. Consider less expensive incentives: a clothing allowance if you have a dress code; pay for internet access, especially if your employees ever work from home; upgrade some software on their computer; sharpen their saw blades if you have a carpenter crew. Those little bits and pieces add up in price, so make sure you don't lose sight of *Alligator Ally*. But they also add up in terms of good will and loyalty. And they are more memorable that a .20/hr raise.

- Train your employees. There are at lease two reasons why this is good creative compensation.

    1. Everyone wants to learn more and improve their skill sets. When you provide your employees with opportunities to learn you show that you care about their personal and professional success. Whether it's

allowing them to take paid time off to attend a conference or paying for a specific training or certification, learning keeps people engaged and they feel appreciated.

2. Trained employees are better employees. Any kind of training, even if it's done in-house, gives your employees a competency edge. That is always good for your business.

## Why Are So Many Employees Dissatisfied With Their Jobs?

Earlier in this chapter we saw that about 50% of business owners were not happy with their employees. Well, it appears that in many cases, the feeling is mutual.

According to a story on CNBC (*August, 2012*), about 60% of *workers* are dissatisfied with their jobs, even in cases where compensation was not an issue. As many as a third are looking to change their job. Isn't that interesting? Employees are as dissatisfied with their bosses as the bosses are dissatisfied with the employees. Maybe there is a relationship between these two points of view.

It's not your responsibility to make sure everybody gets everything they want. But, it is your responsibility to pay attention to whatever undermines a competent, stable workforce.

Unhappy employees cannot possibly be their most effective. And complicating the issue for you is the fact that about 50% of a person's waking hours are spent at work. What chance do you have that your employees will have your back when they are so miserable?

---

**When work sucks, life sucks.**

---

Can you really operate a successful company when your employees dread coming to work every day?

If the things that irritate your employees become pervasive enough, your best employees will go elsewhere. You're not being a softy by paying attention to these irritants. You are being smart and you are protecting your investment.

The good news is that many things that people don't like about their jobs are policy issues or procedures. And it's often pretty cheap to deal with these irritants.

## Not Necessarily DEADLY, but definitely DETRIMENTAL

Some issues will not *necessarily* kill your business, but they can sure make it all harder. And if you get enough of these going on at the same time, they can indeed kill your business.

It's worth pointing out that almost all of these issues can be dramatically improved by good, effective communication between you and your employees. It's equally important for you to understand that "communication" isn't simply a matter of you saying things to them or issuing memos. It's a matter of *them* actually *believing* what you say. and then you listening to *their* response.

## Detrimental Issues You ~~Can~~ Should Positively Impact

Employees Not Knowing What To Expect. Military boot camp, among other things, is a mind-wrecking experience of having to constantly respond to unexpected situations. A good process for molding our nation's finest, but a total pain as a process for managing your staff. When people don't know what is expected of them, they enter into a survival mode. Worse still, they become suspicious and restrained.

*The surest way to turn your employees into adversaries is to keep them guessing about their jobs. Employees care most about their job security and fairness. Curve balls destroy both.*

Employees Feeling Unappreciated. Nobody wants to feel like they don't matter. Regardless of what you think or say, feeling unappreciated is repeatedly communicated through the things YOU do. How you treat people on a routine basis or the kinds of fringe benefits you provide are powerful messages that get communicated throughout your organization 24/7. Feeling unappreciated becomes its own

73

issue that trumps most other issues. It <u>will</u> take on a life of its own.

*It's not just whether your employees <u>are</u> appreciated, it's whether it <u>appears</u> that way! If people don't perceive it, then for them it might as well not exist. Find ways to let your staff know you appreciate them.*

<u>Being "Hung Out To Dry"</u>. When you allow customers or work associates to hassle or disrespect your employees and you don't do anything about it, THAT really sucks. Responding to customer feedback is so important that there is a whole chapter devoted to that topic (#4 – Customer Service). But that's <u>not</u> what we're talking about.

*Any time you allow an employee to be <u>unfairly</u> treated you run the huge risk of losing the respect of all of your employees. On the other hand, standing up for your employees is a great way to solidify Authoritative Power.*

<u>Stuff not working</u>. It may be true that duct tape holds the universe together. But if you have to use it to hold the copier together, it's a real problem. Not having the right tools to operate your business is a MAJOR barrier to the very survival of your business. That is a good enough reason for you to deal with stuff not working. Equally important, nothing drives employees crazy more than having to repeatedly do a task without the proper resources.

*This is particularly true with those seemingly insignificant things that irritate people day after day. Dripping faucets, flickering lights, and offensive smells are a few examples. Easy and cheap to fix, really appreciated. And it communicates that you <u>appreciate</u> your employees*

<u>Throwing a Pity Party For Yourself.</u> As we've already seen, the business of small business is a tough adventure, fraught with breakdowns and bad days. But this is a choice YOU made. Those people who work for you didn't make that choice. They chose to get a job. So they don't want or need to hear the tales of woe that keep you up at night. In fact, most of them don't care.

*When you complain to your employees about how hard your life is, you run the risk of looking like a whiner, or someone who is in over their heads. And when they begin to doubt you have the chops to run your business your Authoritative Power erodes because you appear to no longer have the power to <u>reward</u> your employees for their hard work. (Now you can see why Authoritative Power is one of the inferior powers).*

<u>Having To Make Excuses To Customers.</u> When your employees have to justify why <u>you</u> aren't doing what you said you create a major stress factor AND you destroy your personal credibility with your employees. Even in the best run business, there are times when you can't get something done. But an unhappy customers <u>will</u> take it out on the messenger. Putting people in that situation when they have no control over circumstances is unfair.

*Worse, they could be siding with your customers! Think about that. Would you do business with a dry cleaner or yard care service whose employees criticized their own business? NOT!*

<u>Too Much Drama</u>. When the size of the team is only 5 or 6, everybody gets to know each other way better than if the team had 100 people. And when we say "know" we mean get involved in every level of each other's lives. Such closeness can be a powerful asset, but it also lends itself to squabbling and personal conflicts. NEVER get involved in, or tolerate, such distractions. If <u>you</u> become part of the drama, you literally force your employees to take sides. That can never be a good thing for your business.

*If that drama is caused by you showing favoritism, you elevate the Detrimental Quotient by about ten-fold.*

<u>Job Suitability</u>. Different people are good at different things. And, more importantly, they are *naturally* good at certain things and virtually incompetent at others. Some people are detail-oriented, others are fly-by-the-seat-of-their-pants. Do you really think that a fly-by-the-seat-of-their-pants person is the right pick for your bookkeeper? And do you really think that a fly-by-the-seat-of-their-pants person would *enjoy* the detail-oriented demands of being a bookkeeper?

*Your job is NOT to make everybody happy. But requiring people to do jobs and tasks that they are <u>not</u> suited for undermines their ability and willingness to do a good job for you, and that hurts your business. It's not about trying to make everybody happy, it's about trying to make everybody <u>effective</u> at doing the job you are paying them to do.*

**Most Companies Don't Set Out To Deliver Bad Customer Service.**

In fact, if you ask the typical business owner how they would rate their Customer Service, they probably have a pretty high opinion of themselves. They may even have one of those nifty signs in their office or showroom that say something like

*"We Are Committed To Excellent Customer Service"*

But simply saying it don't make it so. Like many mistakes we make in small businesses, it isn't a matter of *intending* to deliver bad customer service, it is a matter of not realizing that is what you are doing.

> **Bad Customer Service Is A Big Time**
> **BROKEN AGREEMENT**

**What Exactly Is Customer Service?**

Contrary to a popular business mantra, the customer is NOT always right. But the customer IS always the customer. And if you are in business you obviously need customers. The only reason those customers tolerate mediocre products or services is because they don't have a choice, or they aren't aware that they have a choice. Once they become aware that there are alternatives, you can bet they will take them.

Customer Service is a great equalizer and a powerful value-added reason for people to do business with you. While you cannot compete with multi-million dollar companies in a lot of ways, you can totally dominate them in the area of customer service.

**Customer Service.**

1. Doing what you say they will do, and doing it all

2. Delivering products/services/promises on time

3. Ensuring the quality of the products/services you deliver.

4. Taking care of your customers.

5. Taking care of your suppliers.

6. Keeping your business viable and profitable.

## Reasons You Don't Have Good Customer Service

1. Your employees don't have the necessary power to deliver it

2. Your employees don't have the necessary resources to provide it

3. You don't reward good customer service, or punish bad customer service.

*If one or more of these conditions exist, you won't have good customer service.*

## Great Customer Service Is Not A Checklist, It's A Mindset!

Do a search on Amazon.com and you'll come up with almost 90,000 books about how to deliver great customer service. And if you read any of those books, you would probably agree with every point made.

But that is not the problem. Poor customer service is <u>not</u> because you don't know what to do, it <u>is</u> because you are not committed to taking the necessary actions to do it. Really? Everyone knows that customer service is a necessary and good practice, right? Perhaps, but if you are committed to great customer service, you will be already be delivering great customer service. If you have problems with your customer service, it is primarily because you are not sufficiently committed to it.

## Customer Service Is A Result Of Your Company Hairball

**Quality** **Hairball**

*(See "The Hairball", page 7)*

As we've seen, every day you make *dozens* of decisions about how to operate your business. And each decision produces some result or reaction, each of which becomes a "hair". As we've also seen, left on its own, your hairball evolves into its own reality and defines <u>everything</u> in your business, including your <u>real</u> customer service philosophy.

**Most of your Customer Service decisions are made long before you ever have a problem with a customer.**

Most are automatic and don't seem all that important in he moment. How you answer the phone, how clean you keep your place of business, how quickly you respond to questions … in other words, the everyday operation of your business on every level creates and REINFORCES your Customer Service philosophy.

> *How you treat the people you deal with every day is how you will treat your customers.*

By the time you have a problem with a customer, that problem is actually a result of hundreds of "hairs" that have been accumulating over time. That particular problem is actually a result of your business philosophy, aka, your *hairball*.

Consider this. Champion athletes don't have to *decide* each day whether they are going to be champions. They only have to decide *how* they are going to accomplish it. Customer Service is like that. Once you commit to it, the way a champion commits to being a champion, it becomes a matter of *how* to do it better.

## Why Consumers STOP Dealing With Businesses

*Source: Intelligent Dialogue, Bristol*

**55% - had a problem or complaint which was not handled satisfactorily.**

**20% - business was difficult to deal with.**

**17% - found a cheaper deal.**

**13% - found a better price,** *BUT wouldn't have looked if they had been happy with the service.*

> *A single dissatisfied consumer will ultimately tell between 9 and 15 people about their experience. About 13% of them will tell <u>more than 20 people.</u>*
>
> Source: White House Office of Consumer Affairs, Washington, DC

**Anybody Can Deliver Good Customer Service When Things Go Well.**

It's how you handle it when things go bad that separate the pros from the back seat drivers.

Let's say you sell computer parts that you buy from Bob's Wholesale Computer Parts Company. You pay good money for those parts. And you work hard to get your customers to buy these parts from you, and your customers like buying those parts.

Good ol' Bob has even given you permission to put your company logo on those parts. Woo Hoo! Rock on. To your customers, you and the parts are painted with the same brush.

Now, if <u>your</u> customer is using <u>your</u> parts (yes, they are YOUR parts now) and something breaks, he will rightly expect <u>you</u> to take care of the problem without a lot of excuses or delays. He wants results.

Granted, you may also be a victim of bad quality from your supplier. But <u>you</u> are still responsible for <u>your</u> <u>customer's</u> satisfaction. Deal with your supplier later.

People who like buying those parts from <u>you</u> want to know <u>you</u> are there for them. When things go wrong, they want <u>you</u> to fix it. They want you to fix it NOW.

And never forget, in this day of social media, it is SOOOOO easy for customers to complain about you and <u>your</u> parts. Once those bad reviews start piling up on Angie's List, they will stick on you, not the guy who put those parts together back in Bob's factory. Protect your hard work and reputation. Take care of your customers and demand quality from your suppliers.

**Customer Service ALWAYS Begins With Quality**

You may have completely good reasons for embracing a lower quality of a product or service. After all, not everyone drives a new Beamer and not everyone needs 5-Star service. But, if you are going to back off on quality, you *must* communicate that from the start.

It's a real problem for your customers if you say you are committed to quality but you are not. On the other hand, offering lower quality for a lower price can be exactly what your customers want. Just be honest about it.

---

**VALUE = getting the desired benefit for a good price**

"Desired benefit" and "good price" are subjective perceptions that your customers decide. Your job is to provide whatever level of *value* you promise.

---

There is a big difference between being COMMITTED to quality and being INTERESTED IN quality. Someone who is

**Interested in Quality -** allows excuses and circumstances to get in the way of delivering it.

**Committed to Quality -** may not succeed 100% of the time, but will not be deterred by circumstances and will not be satisfied with excuses.

Whatever the level of quality you promise for your business, fulfilling that promise is the first step in providing great Customer Service. Don't make promises you can't keep. If you make them, keep them.

Do you remember the discussion we had in Chapter 2 about "Agreements"? You have made an agreement with your customers regarding quality. Whether it is specifically spoken, or (*shudder*) implied, that agreement is front and center every time your customers spend money with you.

Any BS that comes up around a quality issue is just an excuse to keep from having to honor that agreement. So, don't play that game. Be as good as your promises and your customers will be delighted.

On the other hand, if you fail to keep those quality promises your customers will eventually find an alternative. Wouldn't you?

**A Commitment to Quality Will Make Your Life Easier**

In addition to generally improving your chances of success, having a high standard of quality will make your life a lot easier on many fronts, and it will make your business more profitable.

You may think you don't have enough time to do it right the first time, but you'll end up having to make time to fix it. Or you'll pay the price in unhappy customers. Remember that earlier statistic –

> **55% of the people who stop dealing with your business had a problem or complaint which <u>was not handled satisfactorily</u>.**

Think about that.

**Breakdowns In Quality Take Away Your Ability To Control The Situation.**

Aside from the obvious negative effect this has on your customer and your reputation (remember Angie's List?), you will find yourself having to make concessions that sap your profitability and resources. Operating a business is challenging enough. Don't make it harder on yourself by squandering your money on having to make price concessions for bad quality or bad service.

**"What the heck, it's good enough."**

Do yourself a favor. NEVER tolerate that attitude from your employees or your suppliers. Operate your business as if no detail is too small to manage. The effects of shoddy quality will linger long after the cost is forgotten.

> *Every time your customer uses your product, the quality thing will be right out front, regardless of the price they paid at the beginning.*

Excuses are not going to change that fact, even if they are "legitimate". Success is measured by results, not circumstances. Dissatisfied customers are not repeat customers, and they are not good advertising. In the end, it is a lot easier to apologize for charging a good price for your product or service than it is to apologize for not doing what you promised. (Think about that!)

## Quality ALWAYS Begins With Reliable Resources

When it comes to Customer Service, two essential resources are your employees and your suppliers. There is no way you can do a great job of customer service if either of these is unreliable.

## Your Suppliers: Quality In ➤ Quality Out

The starting point for ensuring that your final product or service is grounded in quality is ensuring that your incoming supplies, inventory and services are grounded in quality. And be prepared to pay for it. Companies that base their philosophy on quality are not usually the cheapest, but they are generally worth it.

Remember, <u>every</u> company (including your supplier) has its <u>own</u> quality hairball. If your supplier has not delivered the quality standard you need, then <u>don't expect them to change!!</u>

Even if they want to, there are as deeply rooted in *their* reasons for doing things as you are! *Their* hairball will determine the level of quality that they are able to provide. It's not up to you to understand and tolerate all the reasons they aren't delivering quality, any more than it is up to your customers to tolerate your reasons for not delivering them the quality they expect.

## Your Employees: The Front Line of Customer Service

When in your entire life have you ever been okay with bad service? Whether it's your waiter in a restaurant, or the examiner at the driver's license office or the mechanic who works on your car, when have you ever thought it was okay to NOT get treated well by the people you are doing business with?

Your employees will absolutely impact your customer's experience of dealing with your company. That's inevitable. The question is whether or not that impact will promote you in a positive way, or will it sabotage your efforts.

## It's Just A Matter Of Time

A great product coupled with indifferent or incompetent service will force your customers to choose between your product and their own sense of fairness and dignity. They may still use you, but they won't like it. They will always be ready to make a switch to one of your competitors if a good enough reason comes up. It's just a matter of time before one of your indifferent employees gives it to them.

On the other hand, employees who really care about their customers and look for ways to serve them become an asset in and of themselves. Your customers will continue to deal with people they like, *even if it's not the best product or value*. In fact, they will seek out great service. It's just human nature. Talk about a secret weapon! When you couple that kind of service with a quality product, BAM!

YOU create the Customer Service attitude of your employees. It doesn't matter what you <u>say</u>, if your employees don't deliver good customer service it is because YOU allow it to happen.

**REMEMBER! You <u>always</u> get what you reward!**

It costs your company <u>6 times</u> as much to get a new customer as it does to keep an existing one. Rewarding (allowing) poor customer service guarantees that you will <u>always</u> be having to replace existing customers with more expensive new ones. What a dumb strategy!

Your company's reputation is enhanced when you deliver great service and it is tarnished when you don't. When your customers talk about your business, <u>their friends and associates listen</u>. If the talk is good, it's the best advertising you can get. If the talk is bad, your advertising can't make up for it. Bad customer service costs you real money.

So, really, why in the world would you not be committed to great customer service? Are you serious about your business or is this just a hobby?

**Quality Is Not A Price Issue**

Having a commitment to quality does not mean that you have to offer only expensive products. If that were true nobody would ever put money in those stupid little gumball machines that give you a two cent plastic ring for 25¢.

The key is <u>value</u>. And value is perceived by the customer. You may personally feel that paying 25¢ for that plastic ring is a total wash, but the kid that gets the ring thinks it's a steal. And if that kid is being a pain in the neck and crying and slobbering, and all it will take to make him feel better is a stupid plastic ring, you may feel that it's a steal, also.

People who only pay $5,000 for a car don't expect to get a fully loaded Porsche. Unless of course, someone convinced them they were getting a fully loaded Porsche. So, if you are going to sell

$5,000 cars, great. Sell the best cars you can and still make a profit. If you give people good value, their desire to be satisfied will be met and you will have fulfilled your quality criteria.

## "Please, don't do me any favors!"

One of the biggest quality problems you're likely to face will come when you try to save money by using sources that offer you a reduced rate in exchange for making some compromise in their normal procedure.

You know the drill:

> *"Tell you what, I'll knock off $200 if you let me work on this in my free time."*

DANGER! WARNING! CAUTION! When you get a cut rate, you can count on getting what you pay for.

When you agree to this type of deal, the other party feels like they are doing you a favor. And if somebody feels like they are doing you a favor, they are not likely to be impressed, nor responsive, if you get impatient.

They do not appreciate what you bring to the relationship. In fact, they might even get resentful! The situation becomes exponentially more complicated if that person is a friend.

In the end, the hidden costs of having something done half-way will totally wipe out whatever savings you thought you made. You must control as many situations as possible if you're going to make your business succeed. SO DON'T GIVE CONTROL TO SOMEONE ELSE!

The temptation will be great, but resisting it will be worth it. Conduct your business with professionals, negotiate fairly, and demand quality treatment. It is your right and it is essential to your survival.

**Growth Almost Always Causes Customer Service Problems.**

Even when growth is planned and generally manageable, the process of expanding of a business is a challenge to maintaining good Customer Service practices. If the growth is uncontrolled, Customer Service will almost certainly suffer.

**This Isn't Mysterious.**

Good Customer Service requires a commitment of time and resources. It must be a high priority in allocating those resources. Any kind of growth, as desirable as it may be from a profitability perspective, often competes for those very resources.

One of the biggest risks associated with business expansion is the risk that you will take your eye off the things that make your business unique and desirable in the first place, because you are focusing your attention on the things that make your business bigger. .

One of the easiest priorities to blow off during growth phases is customer service. And it's not necessarily intentional. It's more a matter of the natural limits that constrain small businesses. Growth requires that you make choices about how you are going to spend your money and focus. If you need to choose between spending time getting the freezer installed in your new restaurant, and spending time calling an irritated customer, you might let the customer slide.

- If you need to promote your evening manager to be the general manager of a new location, you're going to do that, even if the replacement evening manager isn't as good. You'll accept the lower level of competence because you need to promote the growth.

- If you need to squeeze in more service calls for your yard care company because you've expanded your customer base, you are going to reduce the amount of time spent with each existing customer. Little 'extras" are likely to be dropped out or reduced. If you get busy enough, you'll hire some help, and they might not be as good as you are, but you'll accept it because you have to cover the new customers. It takes time to train those new guys, and it takes time to oversee other people's work.

- Adding more taxis to your fleet means adding more oil changes, and probably hiring more drivers. Your cars might not get maintenance as often, and they may not be kept as clean.

If you are the primary Get-It-Done person in your business (most entrepreneurs are), there are limits to how much you can handle without letting something drop out. As desirable as growing your business may be, it increases EVERYTHING in your business, except the number of hours in the day.

Any conversations you have related to growth should always include an objective and honest assessment about what the impact will be on how your customers get treated. As much as you want new customers, you NEED to keep the ones you've got!

*If you fail at that, what's the point of growing in the first place?*

## #5 – Lack of Focus

**What ARE You Doing and WHY Are You Doing It?**

There are plenty of reasons why people start their own business.

- Getting laid off from a job

- Needing to make extra money

- Having a passion for something, seeing a way to do something better, or seeing a way to take advantage of a trend or market force

- Rebelling against the constrictions of working on someone else's agenda

While any of these reasons might explain why you have entered this arena in the first place, none of them explain why people should want to do business with you.  There are millions of restless souls out there who have every bit as good a reason to be in their own business.  What makes you special?

For your business to have the absolute best shot at success, you need to know with certainty what your selling proposition is, whether it is unique or not.  And you need to FOCUS on that proposition.  You must know the answer to the questions:

- **What ARE You Doing?** What exactly is your business purpose?  Specifically, what product or service do you sell?  Who do you sell it to?  How much does it cost?  How much do you make?  If your intention is to cut grass for residential properties, you will have different challenges and goals than if your intention is to provide full-service commercial landscape services.

- **WHY Are You Doing It?** Why did you start this business?  Do you need extra money? Do you need a LOT of money?  Did you get fired or laid off?  Did you always want to do this? It's extremely important to know the answer to this question. If you started your business because you got laid off, it's very likely you will want different things from your business than if you started it because it is a life-long dream.

## The Starting Point For Your Business Was <u>Not</u> The Day You Opened Your Business Checking Account.

It was the day you <u>decided</u> to start your business. On that day, you had a reason, some sort of plan and a vision for the future. And from that moment on, you began to set in place procedures, guidelines and product ideas. If you are like most new entrepreneurs, your business idea has morphed a bit since you first started. Maybe it has morphed a LOT. And maybe that is a big problem for you.

Starting with a clear picture of what you are in business to do, and keeping that picture clear as you go forward, is critical to your success. Based on that picture you need to FOCUS on:

- *what assets you have now*
- *what you can accomplish with those assets,*
- *and what you do best.*

## A Real Life Example

Coca Cola was invented as a fountain drink in 1893, and was bottled in 1894. By the early 1900's it was a great success around the country. Its success inevitably gave rise to a multitude of copycat beverages. For the next decade, soft drink makers engaged in aggressive marketing campaigns, resulting in unique logo designs, bottle shapes, slogans and the first ever celebrity endorsements.

But the marketing tide was shifted decisively for Coca Cola in 1919 when new CEO Robert Woodruff implemented what became a foundation principle of the Coca Cola Company.

He introduced the *focus* of "A Coke within arms length". That simple phrase was the cornerstone of a whirlwind of innovations that defined the world of soft beverages for the next hundred years. Such common ideas as six-packs, vending machines and larger drink bottles are a direct result of that simple focus statement.

This focus succeeded in making it easier for people to drink Coca-Cola at home or wherever they were. Coca Cola became a huge social brand and a big part of people's lives. Not to mention a historical financial success.

## Focus Vs Mission

Any discussion of *focus* must also include a discussion about your company's *mission*. These two concepts are often collapsed into each other, and even used interchangeably, but they are actually two distinctly different components of your overall business operating philosophy.

> MISSION - the <u>context</u> from which you will operate your business. It includes your values, social agenda, commitments to your customers, and the fulfillment of your quality-of-life issues. Your mission statement addresses these issues, even if you have never officially defined them in a mission statement.

---

### Coca Cola's MISSION STATEMENT

*Our Roadmap starts with our mission, which is enduring. It declares our purpose as a company and serves as the standard against which we weigh our actions and decisions.*

- *To refresh the world...*
- *To inspire moments of optimism and happiness...*
- *To create value and make a difference.*

---

> FOCUS - The specific pathway you will take to accomplish your mission. The mission needs to be a durable, *strategic* approach. But focus is a *tactical*

statement that dictates the steps you will take along the way.

---

**Coca Cola's FOCUS**

*A Coke within arms length.*

---

## See The Difference?

### Why Focus Is So Critical

Without a clear focus, you will fall prey to the "Kid In The Candy Store" Phenomenon of operating a business. The "candy" in this case is any opportunity to make a few bucks. As the name implies, you find yourself going from opportunity to opportunity and not putting your attention on any one thing.

Wal-Mart can afford to be all things to all people. You cannot. As you've already learned, it takes a lot more to get your business idea up and running than you thought it would. It takes a lot more work to get people to notice your "better mousetrap". It takes more time to get your product delivered than you expected. In short

---

**The "Two & 1/2 Rule"**

**"It will take twice as much to produce half the result".**

---

Each new product or service you launch in your business WILL take more than you think. So you must learn to choose carefully and keep your attention on what you do best.

### Some Well-Known Examples of Focus

Coffee kiosks – there are over 10,000 stand-alone and drive-thru coffee kiosks that focus almost exclusively on good old coffee, nothing more. (Ex., Seattle's Best)

Baskin Robbins – launched right after World War II, "America's Favorite Neighborhood Ice Cream Shop" was the first specialty ice cream chain and still retains the brand today. Its <u>simple, focused business model</u> makes it one of the most successful food franchise businesses ever.

Jiffy Lube – Founded in 1979 as a dedicated preventative maintenance service center, Jiffy Lube started as an association of 10 stores and has grown to over 2,000 service centers throughout North America and Canada, serving approximately 24 million customers each year. A <u>simple, focused business model</u> has made Jiffy Lube the most successful auto maintenance business line in America.

Redbox – Starting with 11 DVD rental kiosks in Washington Metropolitan Area locations in 2002, Redbox passed 1 billion disc rentals in September 2010. By mid-2011, their kiosks had 36 percent of the disc rental market, compared to only 25 percent for traditional video stores. 68 percent of the U.S. population lives within a five-minute drive of a Redbox kiosk.

Notice the similarities in these very diverse businesses.

- Limited inventory
- Limited manpower
- Low product waste
- High return on product investment
- Low cost of physical footprint
- Flexibility

Training cycles are short, required expertise is limited, and the customer demographic is obvious. If there is an example of "Build it and they will come", these qualify.

**Zero In**

In each of these examples, there is a precise focal <u>point</u> around which these businesses revolve. Some call it a "niche" or a "position".

> **Lack of focus is the single biggest killer of business enterprises in general, and small businesses in particular.**

Sometimes lack of focus is indicated by such symptoms as:
- uncontrolled growth
- not enough money
- overwhelming competition
- low customer satisfaction
- inefficiency operations
- high turnover
- poor quality control

## The Best Indicator That You Are Not Focused

One way that you can tell immediately that you don't have focus is that you feel like your future will be determined by the *circumstances* the business finds itself in, rather than the *vision* that gave birth to the business originally. In that world, there are a lot of factors dictating whether or not your business will prosper OTHER THAN YOU.

Kinda sucks actually. You dedicate your whole life to something just to let someone ELSE decide how it turns out?

Maintaining focus will carry you through rough markets, tight budgets, highly competitive sales demands, and shifts, or even directional changes, in the market place.

There are two objectives to keeping yourself focused.

> 1) It pro-actively points you in the direction <u>you</u> will take your business and,
>
> 2) It informs you how to best utilize your assets.

While it is certainly accurate that entrepreneurs are adept at flying-by-the-seat-of-the-pants, this valuable skill should be used to attack an opportunity, as opposed to being relied upon as a long term navigation approach.

## Ten Pounds Of Stuff In A Five-pound Bag

DO NOT try to figure out how to take all your resources and "focus" those resources in a specific direction.

If you do that, you will find yourself looking for a reason to keep your favorite "thing" in place, what ever that "thing" is (product, tradition, policy, location, etc.).

That is pretty much the same thing as hiring (keeping) an employee because of personal favoritism rather than because of the skills your company needs. Also, pretty much the same result.

## Focus Is A Practical Application Of The Coherence Factor

The whole point of FOCUS is to eliminate the stuff that isn't moving you toward your objective. You do that by clearing stating the TACTIC (*"A Coke within arm's length"),* and then bringing to bear ONLY that which is *coherent with* the tactic.

Failure to focus will cause you to waste time and money, neither of which you will ever have enough of.

## A Tale Of Two Dive Shops

If you ever travel to the Caribbean, you will probably have an opportunity to take a scuba diving excursion. The quality of that experience will depend largely on the vendor you hire to take you diving. Some of the satisfaction will come from the water temperature and weather conditions, of course. But most of it will come from the *experience itself.*

One of the best known dive excursions you can hook up with is operated by UNESCO. These guys are actually an international research organization that does some pretty great things with aquatic life all over the world. In the Caribbean, they focus a lot on coral reefs and dolphins.

Their dive school is an impressive complex of class rooms, equipment stores, restaurants, gift shops and photo centers. The orientation dives take place in a big twenty-foot deep swimming pool with marks and guide-wires strategically placed so you always know exactly how deep you are.

You will have several instructors for your "class", which could be as many as 16 people. Depending on the day of the week, you'll get different levels of experience with your instructors. All of them know how to dive, but all of them don't know how to teach diving very well.

Once you've completed the shallow water (i.e. "pool") orientation, you'll be taken aboard a UNESCO boat out to a reef that is about 30 feet down, and you'll immerse yourself in the extraordinary world of breathing underwater. The cost of your excursion will be between $95 - $120. Most tourists really like the experience, but only about half really LOVE the experience.

## Did We Mention They Have A Gift/Photo Shop?

And you'll probably be able to drop another $30 - $100 on photos and videos of you doing the mermaid thing with all those beautiful tropical fish.

And you can get a commemorative certificate that shows you completed a dive. With a nifty sea-shell frame for only an extra $25.

And they have some really nifty hats and t-shirts you can buy also. Pretty cool, huh?

## Now, Meet Mario.

Mario Cue is a lifetime diver who loves the world of scuba. He runs a little dive shop right on the waterfront in Cozumel. It's called "Tiki-la". Cute, huh?

Mario's shop is pretty primitive by modern standards. The "classroom" is a section of the beach with weathered beach chairs and some tattered umbrellas. His instructors are local divers who use colorful hand-drawn flip charts to teach diving basics. Mario doesn't let just anyone be one of his instructors. They obviously must be certified, but they also must know the intricacies of diving the shallow reefs along the island coastline.

Mario does have a nifty underwater camera and he takes some cool pictures of his diving clients underwater, but instead of printing them out for you (he doesn't have a photo printer in the upstairs bar), he e-mails you the pix at no charge.

A dive class at Tikila will cost you about $45 for the shallow dive (about 20 feet deep), and a bit more if you want to take a boat out to the deeper reefs (30 – 50 feet). Most people are just fine with the shallow dives, especially first-timers. And everyone who takes a class at Tikila <u>loves</u> the experience.

**Mario vs. UNESCO**

There is absolutely nothing wrong with doing the UNESCO dives. But there is also nothing wrong with Mario's version. Many beginning divers prefer it. It's more personal, very quaint and costs less. And you still get the total dive experience.

It would be difficult if not impossible for a local vendor like Mario to compete head to head with a dive operation like UNESCO. And it would be financially deadly to try and offer all the "extras" that UNESCO offers (video, t-shirts, etc.) But, obviously, he doesn't have to. By focusing on what he does well with the resources he has NOW, Mario does just fine.

***Take A Lesson From Mario***

1. FOCUS ON what you can do well, right NOW. Mario focuses his efforts on providing a great diving experience and leaves the gift shops to someone else.

2. FOCUS ON the <u>resources</u> you have right NOW. Old beach chairs on the sand are just as good as classrooms and dive pools.

3. If you do decide to invest in additional resources, STAY OUT OF ALLIGATOR ALLY!! (Go back and carefully read Chapter 1 before you spend money.)

**FOCUS Allows <u>You</u> To Reduce <u>Your</u> Learning Curves**

Every new thing that you bring into your business requires some learning curve. Whether it's a printer for your computer or a new product/service you are offering, there is some period of time that needs to be invested in learning about that thing. Obviously, the time spent learning is not very efficient in terms of producing the ultimate result.

- Every time you introduce a new marketing objective, you invoke a learning curve of some kind.

- Every time you start selling a new product or service, you invoke a learning curve for how to acquire, distribute and support that product.

- Every time you change a policy or procedure within your business, there is a period of time where you, your employees and your customers must acclimate to the new policy or procedure.

Sometimes, it isn't obvious that you are launching a new learning curve. So you need to pay attention. Learning curves are happening all the time. That's why we appreciate experience. It usually means that the learning curve is over, or a least greatly reduced.

Keeping your business focused, and achieving maximum effect from the resources you already have, reduces the number of learning curves you launch.

A normal part of traveling the learning curve is that you make mistakes. Goes with the turf. While YOU may give yourself a bit of slack due to the fact that you are just learning, if one of those mistakes has a negative impact on a customer, it becomes a "hair" in the hairball.

No single hair, but if there are enough of them …

**Any Time You Commit One Of The Mistakes In This Book, You Cause Incoherence.**

- Wasting money, especially when it gets you into Alligator Ally, eliminates needed resources and forces you to deal with problems that have nothing to do with operating your business.

- In the chapter on Agreements we saw that saying one thing and doing something different creates suspicion and resentment. It creates a negative energy that is in DIRECT OPPOSITION to what you want for your business.

- Having poorly trained and unmotivated employees sabotages your efforts at so many different levels. And remember, the smaller your business is, the more disruptive a problem employee can be.

- Not providing good service to your customers can negate everything you did to get them to be customer in the first place.

*Incoherence is more decisive in determining what you can accomplish than ALL of your experience, talent, and hard work!*

---

**Here's Something Worth Wondering About.**

*What if the secret to creating a profitable and fulfilling business is a matter of creating coherence rather than working harder?*

*What if all there really is to do is understand, and then deal with, the invisible interruptions that are sabotaging your efforts?*

*Maybe it doesn't have to be such hard work to make your business successful. Maybe you just need to pay attention to what is going on around you.*

***Choose a point that you can impact, and then build your business around being impactful.***

---

### Your Business Mission Statement – Do You Need One?

Whether you specify it or not YOU need to know what you are in business to accomplish. Otherwise, you will spin your wheels on tactics that never seem to click for you. One way you can tell that you haven't clarified your business mission is that keep introducing new learning curves.

One important value of a mission statement is that it narrows the breach, so to speak. Theoretically, if you have a mission statement, you will make decisions that are inside the scope of that statement. Consequently, you limit the options you allow for yourself.

But a mission statement is, by design, a statement of *philosophy* more than it is a statement of action. It addresses the legacy you want your company to create. In order to create a mission statement you must address the broad outline.

Look again at Coca Cola's Mission Statement:

---

### Coca Cola's MISSION STATEMENT

*Our Roadmap starts with our mission, which is enduring. It declares our purpose as a company and serves as the standard against which we weigh our actions and decisions.*

*•To refresh the world...*

*•To inspire moments of optimism and happiness...*

*•To create value and make a difference.*

---

Notice the part that says:

*"It ... serves as the standard against which we weigh our actions and decisions."*

Obviously, this mission statement speaks about a noble culture. *Refresh the world... inspire moments of optimism and happiness... create value and make a difference.* It is the backdrop against which actions are taken.

But you MUST have a pathway to accomplish that mission, and that pathway needs to FOCUS on what you can do now with the resources you have NOW.

---

### Coca Cola's FOCUS

*A Coke within arms length.*

---

## Keep Your Hairs Focused!

Remember, your business hairball is in play from Day One. Every action you take becomes a hair, and there comes a time when the hairs glom together to become a powerful force in driving your business. By keeping your hairs <u>focused</u>, your emerging hairball will evolve into a force that is driving your business in the direction you want it to go.

## <u>Focus</u> On Your Strengths

When operating a small business, especially for the first time, it is a fact of life that you will encounter situations that are new and unfamiliar to you. Consequently, you will be forced to learn as you go. With a BIG learning curve, you can't possibly know exactly what to do every time. Mistakes are inevitable.

But remember, this book isn't about being perfect, it's about minimizing the number of mistakes we make.

And you will probably make <u>fewer</u> mistakes when you are working in areas that you are naturally good at. On the other hand, you are most likely to mess something up when you are learning how to do something that you are NOT good at.

### Mistakes = Breakdowns = Hairs

Focus on your *strengths*, NOT your weaknesses. In fact, stop thinking about them as weaknesses. They are simply not your strengths – they are *non-strengths*.

If someone tells you that you need to get organized, and you're not good at being an organized person, then you need to understand this truth:

### You Will Never Be Good At Being Organized!!

No amount of classes, no number of consultants, no expensive day-planner, NOTHING will make you good at being organized. NOTHING! If it was in your wheelhouse to do those things they would already be in place.

You already have to learn a ton of new things just to keep your business afloat. Don't add to the weight by trying to force yourself to pick up skills you aren't suited for.

DO NOT ignore areas that are important to your business. You are responsible for EVERY area of your business, including those that you are not naturally good at, i.e., your strengths. But,

---

**There is a big difference between *managing* a non-strength, and *mastering* a non-strength.**

---

It might not be easy, but you will serve your business much better if you keep your attention on the things you do well and acquire the people or resources you need to manage the things you don't do well. Find a way to *compliment* your strengths.

ABOUT EMPLOYEES:
Your resources are limited. Don't waste them on people that do not compliment your strengths.

## A Few Other Things

1.  Anticipate failure but KEEP TRYING. Remember, there is a learning curve in determining your FOCUS. Some things will fit, some won't. Be prepared to keep a critical eye on how things are going and cut loose that which is not consistent with your focus.

2.  Don't deny yourself. All work and no play makes Jack a dull boy and saps his creative energy and makes him unable to understand his employees or other people he deals with. You've got to give yourself time to recharge your batteries. Your business requires it.

3.  Track your progress. Seems pretty obvious, huh? But, if you don't know how something is working, you can't know if it fits.

4.  Take care of your body. Your physical stamina and balance are essential to whatever you are doing. Add little bits of physical activity into your daily or weekly routine.

5. Pay attention to the fuel you are giving your body and your mind. If your business is so demanding that you can't properly feed yourself, how can that possibly be a good thing? NEVER sacrifice you health for your business.

---

1. **FOCUS on what assets you have now**

2. **NEVER promise to do anything that cannot be accomplished with those assets**

3. **ALWAYS focus on what you do best.**

---

## #6 – Not Knowing How You Make (and Lose) Money

### A Couple Of "Laws" You Should Know About

<u>Law of Designer Dust Balls</u>

This Law applies when you fall prey to thinking that a "serious businessman" should offer an expansive catalog of services or products even if you must to invest in slow-moving merchandise. The Law states that if you unwisely invest your resources in accumulating slow moving inventory, the only thing you will have to show for it is an expensive coating of odd-shaped dirt (dust balls) on top of everything.

<u>Law of Stupid Charities</u>

This Law applies when thinking that it is okay to sell stuff that doesn't make any money if it helps "get your foot in the door". This Law says that if you don't make a profit on <u>everything</u> you sell, the net result will be that you have simply bought and sold products for the benefit of your supplier and your customer. But nothing for you.

Both of these Laws are broken by small business owners because they don't fully understand their money machine, After all, there is NO WAY you would intentionally start a business that was supposed to lose money on its products, would you?

### Your Money Machine

Whatever OTHER reason there may be for you owning a business, the bottom line is that your business must make money. For some people, making a lot of money is the whole point. For others, making enough money to do what you want to do is sufficient. Either way, the operative word here is "money" and it is the fuel that runs your business.

Imagine an oil derrick. Once it gets going, it continuously pumps oil, day after day, until it runs out. It's an oil-pumping machine.

Your business is like that, or at least it is when it's working right. You are not extracting oil from the ground, you are extracting money from our economy.

That part is obvious. But there is a refinement to the Money Machine that seems to escape many small business owners.

## It Ain't SPENDING money unless it's YOUR money!

The definition of YOUR MONEY:

*The money left over AFTER you pay for the cost and delivery of the goods.*

There are many things you can do with Your Money.

- Pay Bills
- Pay Employees (including YOURSELF)
- Buy Stuff For Your Business
- Expand Your Business

Having a bunch of YOUR MONEY is a good thing!

### The Difference Between <u>Cash Flow</u> and <u>Your Money</u>

Consider a product that sells for $7.

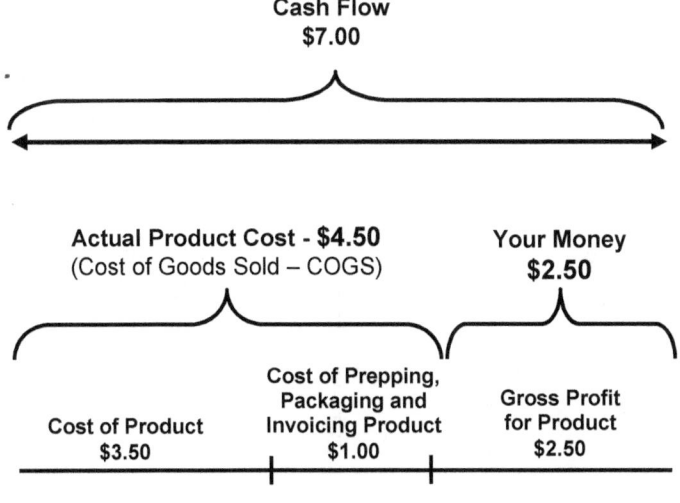

If you spend <u>any</u> of the money that is NOT Your Money, then you are spending <u>Beta</u> Money. Remember, Beta money is money you don't yet have, *but plan to have (or hope to have)*.

In this case you are spending the money needed to pay for the cost of your goods as if it was your money, but it's really not YOUR money. It actually belongs to *Mr. Cost-Of-Goods*. At some point, you will need to give Mr. COGS his portion. So, you can't count that portion as *Your Money*. If you have already spent that portion on something else (payroll, 941 taxes, utilities, etc.), then you spent Beta money.

> ***No Time for Self-Deception.*** *If you are spending Beta money, recognize that is, in fact, what you are doing.*
> *No matter how justified it is to spend Beta money, <u>the bill always comes due</u>. Often when you can least afford it.*

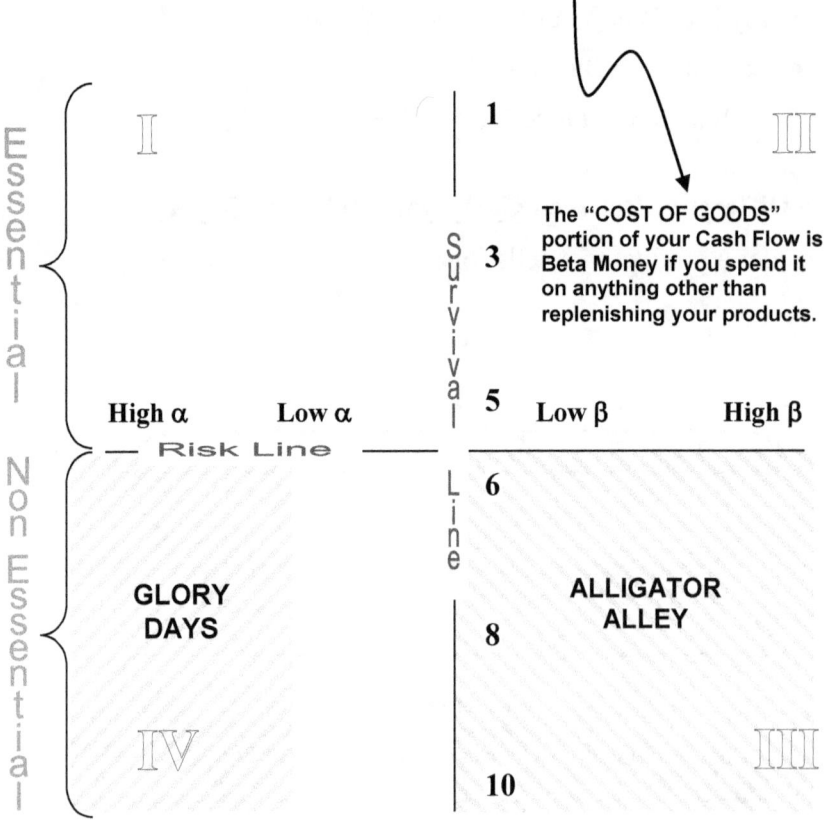

**Money Is Essential To Your Business Survival**

**You Must Know -**

> **What IS Making You Money, and**
> **What IS NOT Making You Money.**

---

**3 Things That Need To Happen Any Time**
**A Business Transaction Is Done**
(in addition to the *Agreement* issues
we discussed in Chapter 2).

1. You need to make a profit

2. You need to satisfy your customer

3. You need to satisfy your supplier

Take away any one of these elements and you cannot
sustain your business. And it won't matter what reasons
you have for the take-away.

---

**It All Starts With Your Price (Duh!)**

There are a lot of factors that should be taken into account when
you are establishing price. Before you can determine anything
else, you absolutely must know how much it costs you to get
your product IN AND OUT the door, and how much profit you
need to make each time you sell that product.

If the difference between those two figures is not sufficient to
provide you with enough money to operate your business, then
you are wasting your time selling that product. (Refer back to
*The Law Of Stupid Charities* earlier in this chapter).

**Know The Value of Your Product** – Your product is the source
of income for your business. The price you charge for your
products and services is critically important. And so is the actual
cost of delivering those products. You might be thinking this is
pretty obvious, but it is one of the most common mistakes made
in operating a small business.

In Chapter 1, we looked at how you spend your money. But you
gotta have money to spend. Yes, you will encounter

circumstances that require you to take a loss in order to keep your promises to customers or suppliers. It goes with the turf of being a 95%-er.

But it should <u>never</u> be an operating strategy to run your business that way.

---

*The story you are about to read is true. The names have been changed to protect ... well, you'll see why the names have been changed.*

### Robbing Peter And Kicking Paul To The Curb

Stan was the manager of the U.S. office of a British company that manufactured soil testing equipment. He was responsible for securing a $50,000+ order which was going to be shipped overseas.

On the surface this was extraordinary. $50,000 was, at the time, more sales volume than this company usually generated in three months. But after adding up the costs of securing the products, packaging them for overseas shipment, and paying to get them where they were going, the net margin on this sale was a <u>minus $7,000</u>! It wasn't Stan's first mistake, but it was the proverbial straw that broke the camel's back. He was fired.

To this very day you can probably still hear Stan raging about what stupid people those Brits were for firing the guy who generated more <u>sales volume</u> than anyone in the history of the US subsidiary of that company.

He never got past the <u>sales volume</u>. It doesn't matter if he sold a million dollars worth of products. If his company lost even $10 on the deal, then it was a bust and should never have happened.

---

# Do not allow yourself to be seduced by IMPRESSIVE SALES VOLUMES that return small margins.

There will be times when, in spite of your best efforts, you will still make this mistake because you didn't have the right information. Alas, that is an unfortunate consequence of learning what works. Hopefully, you won't do it often, but you will do it.

*Don't make matters worse by doing it when you don't have to.*

## LOW MARGINS: The Achilles Heel of the 95%-er

Business 101 teaches us that a business survives on income, <u>not revenues</u>. Revenues describes all of the money your business brings in, and income describes that portion of the money that you can use after you pay for your products (after subtracting COGS). Revenues is a glossy, much abused word, that generates awe and excitement. It can also be the worst possible motivator, and an even worse justification for spending money you could use elsewhere.

Another phrase that describes the difference between revenues and the cost of your product is your "Gross Margin". This is the actual amount of money you can use to run your business. All of the costs associated with your business, from stationary to rent to payroll, must come out of your Gross Margin.

## No, You Didn't!

There are a lot of reasons why otherwise intelligent business owners choose to sell at low margins.

- Optimistic predictions that, once you "get your foot in the door" you'll then be able to sell everything else at killer prices, is probably the biggest misconception. Also known as "The Tragedy of The Loss Leader".
- The belief that low prices generate high volumes and the result is more money. HA!

- At some point we have all heard, or said, things like,

  *"I had to cut the margin to make the sale",*

  *"This is a good customer, I have to treat them special",*

  *"We'll make up the difference in kick-backs from the manufacturer".*

At the end of it all, whatever your reasons, the net result is you reduce the amount of YOUR MONEY coming into your business. That logic may work for companies with deep pockets, or those whose paycheck doesn't rely on being profitable month after month.

## Selling Products At Low Margins ALWAYS Hurts Your Business

Right at the top of the list is the obvious fact that you have to do more work to make the same amount of money. Why in the world would anyone want to do more work to make the same amount of money? You may be thinking that it isn't really more "work", since you really just have to move more volume.

But there are significant hidden dangers in relying on increased volume to make enough money. Higher volume requirements have their own cost, in people, space and higher operating capital. Higher product levels mean:

- Higher insurance coverage

- More complicated inventory system

- Often requires expanded or improved infrastructure in your business

- Ties up your cash or your credit lines because you have to sink a larger percentage of your income into inventory.

- Stresses your resources to provide quality control and customer service. After all, more volume ALWAYS means more breakdowns.

The last thing you want to do when you are operating a small business (especially a start-up) is give yourself more potential headaches.

## Besides, It Doesn't Really Work That Way

It is a common mistake to think that lower prices automatically translate into higher volumes. It's the Small Business version of that old saying "Two can live as cheaply as one." Doesn't work when people are getting hitched and it REALLY doesn't work in a small business.

In fact, the process actually works in reverse. Companies that are already doing large volumes can afford to cut prices in response to competition or changes in the market place. Much research has been done which illustrates that price is very seldom a customer's primary buying motivator. More important than price are service reputation, product quality, name identification, access/convenience and customer loyalty. So, whenever possible, don't compete on a price basis. Compete in one of the other areas.

Even when you can justify dropping your prices in anticipation of, or in response to, higher volumes, you will still have to do the same amount of work per transaction that you do on higher priced goods. You absolutely cannot sacrifice quality or service. You still have to package, deliver, and get paid for every sale.

## Your Express Ticket To Alligator Ally

If it turns out that you are right, and lower prices actually do result in substantial volume increases, then you will probably need to expand your operation to accommodate the growth. And you will likely have to spend the money on that expansion BEFORE you make the profit from it. Especially after you reduce the "YOUR MONEY" portion of each sale. Unless you have that money in the bank and don't need to spend it on anything else, you'll be spending Beta money on that expansion. Alligator Ally – here we come!

## ROI – Even If The Price You Pay Is Great, How Long Does It Take For You To Get Your Money?

You probably already know this drill. Think about the last time you bought business cards. Did you fall for the "I saved money in the long run" logic? Yeah you know that you spent more than you needed to, but you really saved money buying 1000 cards instead of 500 because you only had to pay another $10 to double your number … blah, blah, blah.

Happens all the time. Not so big a deal if you're tying up $50 in some business cards you'll never use. Way bigger problem if you tie up $1,000 on inventory that will take you 12 months to sell.

> *Tying up your money in a slow-moving item for a long time can be as bad as not giving yourself the money in the first place. And as deadly.*

And obviously, this is even more critical if your product has a short shelf life, like flowers or baked goods.

### Gimbel's Folly Will Kill <u>You</u>.

Back in the hey days of the great retail giants (Macy's Gimbel's, Sak's), Barnard Gimbel famously said,

> *"I know half of my advertising works. I just don't know which half".*

The dilemma came to be known in marketing parlance as "Gimbel's Folly". You throw everything at the wall and some of it will stick. Now, if you are worth BILLIONS of dollars such a folly is just that, a folly. But if you are a 95% -er, such thinking is certain death.

### Know Which Of Your Products Are Making You Profit And How Much<u>.</u>

Your time and money are at a premium in a small business. Squandering those precious and limited resources on unprofitable activity is the surest path to becoming just one more of the MILLIONS of statistics about business failure.

> **It's way easier to apologize for charging a fair price than it is to apologize for poor quality or service because you don't make enough profit.**

## One Of The Best Way's To Make Money Is to Know WHAT You Are Selling

We've all had the experience of asking a sales clerk about a product's features and they don't know. Or worse, they tell you something inaccurate or outright wrong.

It doesn't matter what you are selling, you need to have a competent working knowledge of the product, its warranty, sizes, colors, prices, etc. And so does everyone who must deal with the customer about that product.

We already know from the chapter on Customer Service that you need product competence just to take care of your customers, but there is an important "profit motive" in having a competent sales staff.

## When You Know Your Product, You Know Your Customer.

And you also know what ELSE they might need that addresses their interests. It's called UP-SELLING. And it can only happen if the person making the sale knows WHY the customer might be interested in that product.

For example, if you know why a person is interested in a paint brush, you can inquire about a whole product line of other items. But if you don't know why a person would buy that item, or why certain paint brushes are used for different paint tasks, you must rely entirely on what your customer knows and there is no possibility of up-selling unless the customer thinks of it.

Furthermore, if the customer wants to know why one paint brush is twice as expensive as another, and you can't explain it, then you probably won't sell the more expensive item (with a bigger margin!). You might even lose that customer in the future.

## Getting Your Foot In The Door Doesn't Matter If You Can't Up-Sell.

Earlier in this chapter we looked at the reasons you might choose to sell products at low margins. One of the most popular is "To get your foot in the door". But if you don't know enough about your product to up-sell, getting your foot in the door is just another way of saying "My prices are low!"

Knowing WHAT you are selling, and WHY your customer is buying it, is one of the least expensive, most effective ways you can increase revenues and margins.

> *Some one in your business should know*
> *EVERYTHING, and EVERYONE should know*
> *SOME THINGS about what you are selling*

### He Had A Reason For Stocking 38 Different Draft Beers

The Carolina Ale House is a regional sports bar/restaurant chain based in Wilmington, NC. It is well known for its wide selection of 38 different draft beers. (Talk about a place where you really need to know WHAT you are selling!)

According to the company's story, The Ale House was inspired during a layover in London. Owner Lou Moshakos found himself in a true British ale house and wanted to reproduce the environment back home. He had a reason for stocking 38 different draft beers.

### Do You?

If you were going to open a sports pub, would you need to also sell 38 different brands of draft beer? In fact, if you did sell that product, and you didn't understand the product, or didn't have the appropriate beer delivery system to keep it cold and fresh, or didn't sell enough of each brand to make a decent profit, it would hurt every aspect of your business.

The same principle applies to any product or service you offer. Being a really good trim carpenter doesn't necessarily mean you can also build a deck. Being a great computer techie doesn't mean you understand all the software in that computer. Having the best pizza doesn't mean you should also sell lasagna.

You should always have a good reason why YOU are selling a product or service. If you don't have a good reason, don't do it! Especially if that product is slow-moving.

> *Just because there is an item your customers want doesn't mean it's an item YOU should be selling.*

## The Worst Person To Rely On?

When deciding which products to stock, the person <u>selling you those products</u> may not be your best advisor. No mystery there. That's how they make their money.

One of the best reasons to know why you are selling a product is so you can protect yourself from being talked into buying something you can't resell.

Along those lines,

> **A competent, knowledgeable supplier CAN be a great resource in helping select your products.**
>
> **CAUTION: Just because your competitors are buying something doesn't necessarily mean you should also!**

## Sales Promotions – the DANGEROUS double-edged sword

Sales Promotions are completely different than using specific Promotional Items as a marketing tool.

| Sales Promotions | Promotional Item Marketing |
|---|---|
| Using your existing products to promote your business | Acquiring products (pens, calendars, hats, …) to promote your business |

Since we're talking about how you make money, we can dismiss the "promotional items" process <u>completely</u>. You will NEVER make money off promotional give-aways. Think about it. Do you expect to make money off your business cards?

Promotional items are some of the least effective advertising you can do. So if you are going to do this, keep it cheap and NEVER spend Beta money on this kind of marketing. Never. Never. NEVER! If you can spend YOUR MONEY, great, have fun.

### There Are Good Reasons For Doing Some Kind Of Promotion.

But, one of those reasons should <u>not</u> be that you expect to make money from the promotion itself. And therefore, whatever else you think you are doing, you are essentially spending your money on (hopefully) <u>creating</u> present or future business.

Not a bad reason to spend money. If it works. But according to some studies, not only do sales promotions usually <u>not make money</u>, the vast majority of <u>all</u> promotions actually don't produce any measurable result over time. (There are exceptions, and we'll look at those a bit further along.)

Keep in mind, we're talking about <u>how you make money</u>! Right out of the starting gate you should be skeptical of tying up your resources for <u>any</u> activity that will not make you money.

### Should Spend Money On A Sales Promotion?

First, understand the impact of what you are doing. When you reduce the price of something, you don't reduce the <u>cost</u> of the

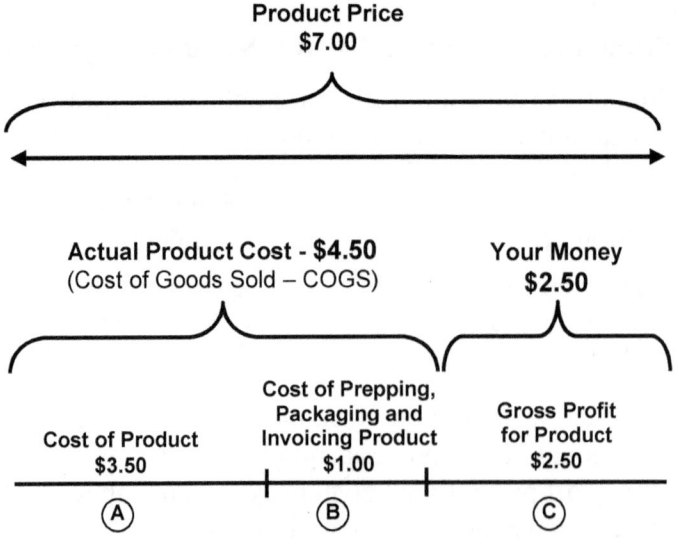

product (A), and you don't reduce the cost of packaging and delivering the product (B). The entire price reduction comes out of your gross profit for that product (C).

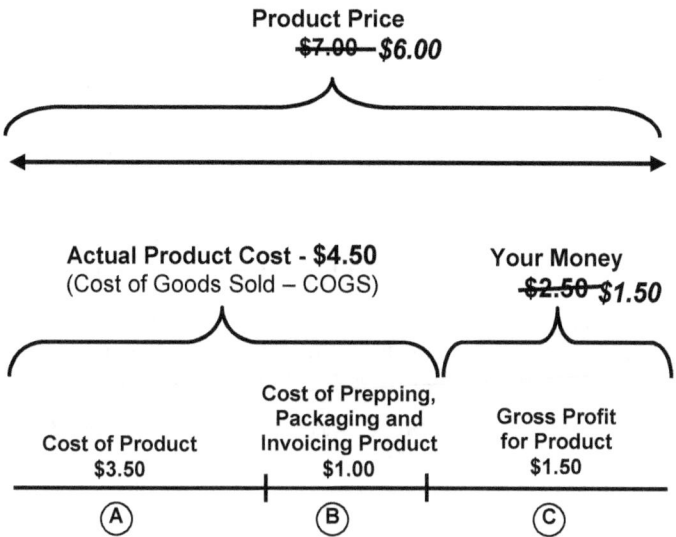

In the example above, if you reduce your selling price by $1.00 (~15%), to lure in customers you are reducing YOUR MONEY by <u>40%</u>. For nothin'!

So, if your promotional item or service has a really high margin, or is clogging up your inventory, then maybe moving that item is a good idea, even if you do cut your margin in half. But any other justification you have is nothing more than turning yourself into a discount house, at least for that product. For nothin'!

### Be Careful What You Wish For

It is possible that you will generate increased levels of interest for <u>that particular product</u>. If your promotion is very successful, you could find yourself committing additional business resources (people, physical space, money, etc.) to supporting the promotion. Do you really want to burden your limited resources for a product with rock bottom margins? Not if you are interested in making money.

## You Can't Go Back

If you do a really good job promoting your product, you better be prepared to keep the promotional price for a while. Customers can get irritated when you suddenly jack up the price of something they have been buying at a lower price. If the product is good enough to draw a lot of customer interest, it is also good enough to illicit bad feelings if you make it more costly to get.

**Is Your Promotion A Good Spending Decision?** *(A perfect use of the Spending Graph.)*

## A QUICK REVIEW OF THE SPENDING GRAPH

*" α" refers to money you have in the bank that you don't have to use for anything else. This is your money. Spend it on whatever you want, including a new office desk, a bonus, or a promotional activity.*

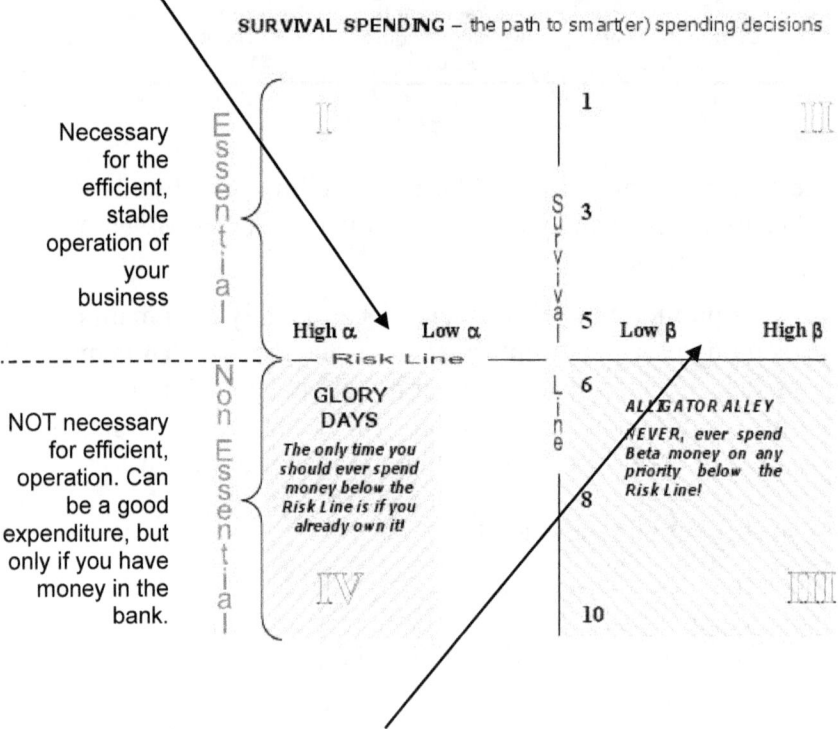

SURVIVAL SPENDING – the path to smart(er) spending decisions

Necessary for the efficient, stable operation of your business — Essential

NOT necessary for efficient, operation. Can be a good expenditure, but only if you have money in the bank. — Non Essential

High α    Low α
— Risk Line —
Low β    High β

**GLORY DAYS**
*The only time you should ever spend money below the Risk Line is if you already own it!*

**ALLIGATOR ALLEY**
*NEVER, ever spend Beta money on any priority below the Risk Line!*

Survival Line: 1, 3, 5, 6, 8, 10

*"Βετα" refers to money you have borrowed, or will have to spend on something in the future. This is NOT your money. Always spend it carefully, and DON'T spend it on Non-Essential expenditures.*

After all other considerations, before you spend any money on promotional activity, know where that money is coming from., *i.e., is it Alpha or Beta money.* Remember, just because you have the cash flow to pay for a promotional activity, that doesn't mean you are spending your money wisely.

> *Promotional Activity of any kind is a high risk/low return proposition. It may be unwise, but it is not necessarily deadly. UNLESS YOU ARE SPENDING BETA MONEY! In that case you are spending money you don't have on something that has a low probability of making you money.*
>
> *Dumb.*
>
> *And Deadly!*

## Only promote items or services that you can afford to give away, or sell very cheaply

Know what you're going to get and what you're <u>not</u> going to get. If the authentic balance between those two worlds works for you AND if you don't have to spend Beta money, go for it and have fun.

### A Call To Action

The best promotions are those that are linked to some action or purchase by your customers. If you give away ink pens or calendars, they are just that: give-aways. They don't make any money. At best they are a trivial attempt at image advertising, but mostly they just scratch an occasional itch. (# gimmick).

But if you give away one-half of a $20 bill and to get the other half the customer must purchase a $200 case of wine, that could work!

## When The "Promotion" Is The Product

There are some businesses that rely on promotional activity as a way of doing business, such as radio, television and magazines. These companies just want to get your attention, because their money is made based on how many people listen, watch or read.

For example, a radio station sells advertising. That's their product and that's how they make money. The price they charge for advertising is based on how many people listen to them. So anything they do to "promote" their station is the whole point of their strategy. In that case, simply getting your attention constitutes a <u>successful sale</u>. They don't need you to do anything else.

But understand the difference. In your case, you are trying to get the customer's attention <u>so you can make a sale</u>. Just getting their attention is irrelevant unless it results in those customers spending more money with you on an ongoing basis. Different ball game entirely!

## A Product Promotion That Works Really Well

Rosetta Stone Inc. is a U.S. software company that sells a computer-assisted language learning program (Rosetta Stone) that teaches more than 30 languages. The program uses a patented "emersion" process that simulates being "immersed" in the language as a way of teaching.

Each language product has 3 levels (hence the name "Rosetta Stone"). Rather than try and explain how their process works, they just give you a free Level 1 tutorial in any of their languages you want to try. In other words, they give away one of their products for free.

But it's not a pen or calendar that just has their name and phone number on it. It's a useful product that addresses the core of what you want. In the process of giving this product away, they gather from you all the customer information any good merchant would love to have.

This promotional strategy would be a vain attempt if the product didn't work. But it does. Very well. And most important, it absolutely leads to up-sells of different products. Of course, if you only wanted to learn Level 1 Spanish and had no desire to learn Levels 2 &3, or if you had no desire to learn any other language, the freebie would be the end of the game. *Which is the case with most promotions.*

But the folks at Rosetta Stone, Inc. have figured out that such a customer is probably not going to bother with getting Level 1 in the first place. They know that if you are interested enough to get their freebie, you are probably interested in more language training. Once you have seen how well Level 1 works for Spanish, you are hooked on the process. And they make it really easy for you to buy something else.

**The Elements Of A Good Promotional Sales Item**

- A useful product (product reviews for Level 1 of the Rosetta Stone programs are consistently overwhelmingly positive)

- Each customer only gets 1 product (not a dozen at discount promotional prices, and not a freebie every time they walk in the door)

- Low Cost to produce (once the initial program is created the cost of making a CD is only a few cents, and a download costs nothing)

- Get something in return (in this case detailed customer info)

- The promotional item itself drives customers to acquire more product.

- The "up-sell" process is easy and built-in.

If your promotional product or activity doesn't do all these things, you should definitely reconsider. Quick. Before you waste money that doesn't make you any more money.

**Reward/Incentivize behavior**

Some promotional tactics are designed to reward or incentivize customers. A good example is a "drink card", where you buy 10 and get the next one free. Not a bad idea, because the customer has to buy products BEFORE you give the promotional item.

Another version of this is "pre-buy" program, where customers purchase a certificate or something that gives them reduced pricing on future purchases. Also can be a good idea, because you are requiring the customer to buy something up front.

But, this one can turn back around and bite you if you don't include the reduced margins on those future purchases in your revenue calculations. If somebody buys that certificate, you've got to honor the reduced purchase, even if it ends up costing you more than you hoped.

Always include an expiration date with ANY promotions.

> *In the end, spending your money on promotional items and activities is mostly an ego trip, not a marketing decision. 95%-ers can't afford to waste money on ego trips.*

## #7 – Not Having An End Game

*Everything that can be counted does not necessarily count; everything that counts cannot necessarily be counted.*

~Albert Einstein

### Knowing When To Call It Quits

For all the reasons we have already discussed, you need to know why you are in this game to begin with. But everything we have discussed in this book is pretty much wasted if you don't know when it's time to go.

It's not necessary to have an end *date*, but you absolutely should have an end *game*. And if you don't know why you started your business, you can't possibly know when, and if, you have achieved the goals you had in starting the business in the first place.

More importantly, you won't even notice when you are so far off course that there's no going back. You won't get to choose your destination.

### The Great Unanswered Question of The Entrepreneur

*How the hell did THAT happen???*

It might seem counter-intuitive to start thinking about shutting it all down before you even get started. After all, we're entrepreneurs! We can do anything! Are you kidding? We don't quit! We're the back bone of America!!

In that world of thinking, you won't even pay attention when your resources max out and new issues start popping up. Or old ones fail to get resolved. Because you have your attention on *yourself*, NOT your *business*.

One of the titans that built America, J.P. Morgan, introduced commercial banking on a scale that had never been seen in the world before.

Contrary to the way things are done today, banking used to be the art of <u>minimizing</u> risk. Morgan believed it was infinitely more important to know when to cut your losses than it was to make a big score. He built an empire on that philosophy, and became one of the richest men in the entire world doing it.

Unless you started your business for the sole purpose of fighting for the sake of fighting, , the surest way to the complete destruction of a small business is to fight just for the sake of fighting (i.e., take unnecessary risk because you bought into the BS that you are supposed to do that).

## "The Drift" – the invisible saboteur

If you don't take "the drift" into account, you can be doing everything else right and still miss the mark by miles.

In sailing terms "the drift" refers to the combined effect of wind, current and water conditions on the actual *location* of a vessel, NOT the actual *direction* the vessel is travelling,

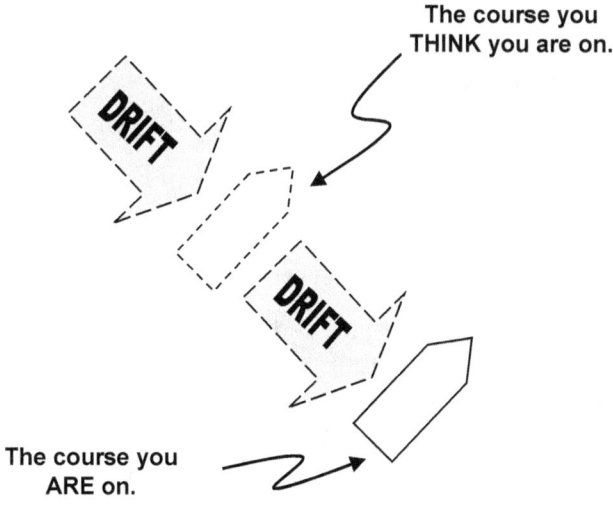

The course you THINK you are on.

The course you ARE on.

Today, of course, we have GPS. 200 years ago, sailors used the stars. Without either of those, you are basically at the mercy of the drift.

In a small business, the drift expresses itself as the day-to-day minutia that you deal with. You respond to everything because you must. Each new challenge, each new accomplishment, each new day you do what you do in response to whatever is in your face.

Your reactions will almost always be money-driven, and we already know how problematical THAT can be. But whether or not they are, when you're in the drift, your reactions will always be REACTIONS.

However you respond, unless you saw it coming and stayed true to your original course, when the dust settles, there is a pretty good chance you will no longer be on the course you were on. And you won't know it.

*You don't keep your word – drift*

*You allow a product to go out your door that doesn't meet your original standards – drift*

*You allow an employee to not keep their word to you – drift*

*Of course the list is endless.*

*The Drift doesn't happen in one fell swoop. By definition, it happens over time and it's <u>not obvious</u>.*


**The Drift Don't Care - Never Underestimate It's Power**

The forces that constitute the drift are indifferent to your objectives or your responses. Like it doesn't matter why the wind is blowing you off course. It just is. Any sailor worth his salt knows you must constantly resort to your star chart or your GPS to ensure you are heading where you want to go.

A brutal storm can blow you way off course in the blink of an eye. But if you are the aforementioned "salt", you will have the resources and the skills to make the necessary course correction.

The very nature of launching your small business places you squarely in the drift. Almost immediately, you will be devoting all of your attention to those things that must be done NOW. The drift will have free reign, and it will take its toll. Left to it's own, it will claim your business as just one more piece of *drift*-wood.

Don't let your business become a piece of driftwood. Unless that's why you started your business in the first place. In which case you have more money than you need, and no reason to be reading this book.

### Your End Game Is Your Star Chart

If you don't have one, or if you don't use it, your ultimate destination will not be of your choosing whether you like it or not.

BTW, the only thing dumber than not having a Star Chart in the first place, is having one and not using it.

**YOUR ENDGAME NEEDS TO TAKE INTO ACCOUNT THE VERY REAL POSSIBILITY (LIKLIHOOD?) THAT YOUR BUSINESS WILL DISAPPOINT YOU.**

### Articulating Your End Game

In order to articulate an authentic End Game, you must have:

A big enough reason to do it

Outcomes you can measure

A reliable way to assess your progress along the way

And <u>that</u> is why you could benefit from

## *A Mission Statement*

You'll recall from our earlier discussion about Mission Statements (*Focus, page 92*) a Mission Statement:

> *"...includes your values, social agenda, commitments ... and the fulfillment of your quality-of-life issues."*

Remember, your Mission Statement is a statement about what you stand for, *what your business stands for!*

While a fortune 500 company needs a mission statement that addresses and *endless* future, you need one that addresses your End Game. It does that by recognizing a fundamental, INCONTROVERTABLE reality that seems to evade the consciousness of most entrepreneurs.

# Your life is not separate from your work!!!

In any given week, there are seven 24-hour days equaling 168 hours. Typical business owners spend:

| TYPICAL ALLOCATION OF HOURS EACH WEEK | |
|---|---|
| 100 hrs | Physically at work, or dealing specifically with work issues, including talking on the phone, checking e-mail, running errands etc. Just because these hours don't fit neatly into a daily schedule doesn't mean they don't happen. |
| 42 hrs | Sleeping. The human body simply can't function on less than six hours per night. (sigh) |
| 26 hrs | For EVERYTHING else. The quality of your life, and the success of your business, will ultimately depend on how effectively you utilize those 26 hours to take care of yourself and your relationships. |

Don't take this as scientific anything. Take it as an overview.

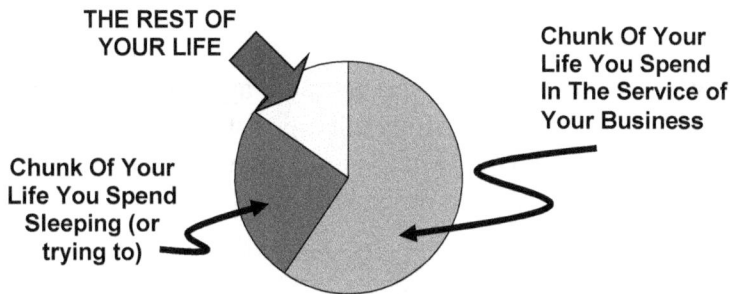

*Well now. Could it be that the <u>truly</u> <u>happy</u> entrepreneur is the one who gets to spend the biggest chunk of life doing what he or she really wants to do, AND GETS PAID FOR IT?! Hmmmmmmmm....*

# YES, THIS HAS EVERYTHING TO DO WITH YOUR END GAME.

**Back to your Mission Statement.**

Once The Drift takes hold, relationships, love, self-expression, the kids, the parents, the friends, the walks in the rain...<u>everything</u> gets put on hold until you ARE NOT WORKING!!!

Problem is, you are pretty much ALWAYS working!

And in the meantime, your <u>life does not</u> get put on hold, it keeps "life-ing" along. Kids grow up, friends mature and develop new interests (and infirmities), and sometimes those great places you used to walk in the rain get paved into parking lots. Life happens on a day to day basis while you are busy trying to get a day off.

## A Mission Statement That Serves Your Life

Answer the following:

1. What do you do when you get to do <u>anything</u> you want to do? Whether it is reading, talking, fishing, exploring or even more working, what you do when you can do anything you want to do is what you LOVE. Pick 2 things.

   *Reading*

   *Sleeping in on rainy days*

2. What are two of your natural strengths? These are traits you don't have to work at, they're just natural. Keep in mind, just because you have a *positive* trait doesn't mean it's natural. You may have worked your entire life to be organized, but just because you succeeded, that doesn't make it *natural.* List natural strengths.

   *Cheerfulness*

   *Organizational skills*

3. Write a very brief description of your version of the perfect life. None of the bad, just the good and plenty of it. Don't hold back, but let's be clear, if your version includes living off-planet, you might be taking this a bit too far.

   *Living right on the beach, out my door, sand in my toes.*

Now, tie all that together in a simple statement. It could be something like this:

*I am going to use my cheerfulness and organization skills, by riding my bike and sleeping on rainy days, to*

*create a life where I get to live on the beach, sand in
my toes.*

Laugh if you must.  But don't ignore the obvious –

> *If you were being truthful with yourself, then the
> farther you are from doing what that statement asks of
> you, the unhappier you will be.*
>
> *And, (this is really painful), if your business does what
> most small businesses do, you will have given it ALL
> up, not just your business, but your life as well.  Now
> THAT really sucks.*

## The Other Obvious Thing (and this is way good) –

Running your own business could be the closest that most of us
will ever get to CREATING our own PERFECT LIFE.

But not if The Drift has its way with ya'.

## You Can't Ride Two Horses With One Ass
*(aka, "You Can Only Serve One Master")*

This isn't either/or and it doesn't happen right now.  It is a
journey, and one that will be shorter than most readers are
expecting.

Like the Ol' Salts and their tall ships.  You set out, you battle
whatever there is along the way, and you pay the price and reap
the rewards for your courage and vision.  But, if any of it is ever
really going to be worth it (according to YOUR point of view),
you MUST stay true to the course.

Which course?

The one that asks you to live your perfect life.

Yes, it is that simple.

## Your Business – The New Boss
*Same as the old boss? That would kinda suck.*

Since you're going to spend the vast majority of your waking hours laboring under the yoke of your new master, wouldn't it be wonderful if such laboring was actually getting you to <u>your</u> perfect life by the swiftest route. Or better still, if such labor was not labor at all in the traditional sense.

Like the guy who loves golf and makes a living teaching it. The bookseller who loves books. The animal lover who opens a vet clinic.

When you find a way to make money doing the thing you love to do, it's like …

> *"You get your money for nothin' and your chicks for free"*
> Dire Straits, *Money For Nothin'*

Sometimes a fine version of that is doing something that is just okay, and it makes okay money, but it allows you to do what you really want to do when you want to. Peachy!

Or maybe there is nothing inspiring about your business. Maybe you launched it as a desperate last measure, or as nothing more than a hopeful alternative to your current reality.

No problem, here. After all, one of the reasons that work force participation drops during hard economic times is because those of us with the chops to strike out don't sit around waiting for our crumbs to be handed down.

However you got there, if your business is going to serve you well, you must have an End Game. And the brutal reality is this:

If you do the Mission Statement exercise, and you can see no way that your current business can get you there, then your End Game from that point forward needs to include shutting down the business you have and starting over.

And lest you think this frivolous, you might as well know. You will either make that call, or the Drift will make it for you. Either way, it gets made, And you live with the result. FOREVER.

# APPENDIX

## MERLIN'S SPENDING GRAPH
*Merlin's Spending graph was introduced in "Wasting Money" (page 22). Use these examples to more clearly understand how to use the Spending Graph and what it can tell you.*

### Is It A Good Spending Decision?

### Spending Example 1:  Buying a new copier.

Maybe you don't absolutely *need* a new copier, but the old one breaks down a lot (meaning you have to keep spending money on service calls) and it makes cruddy copies.  You do your homework and find that you can get a good machine that will reliably handle your needs for only $1,500, and you have that much in the bank **(A).**

This is probably a sound business move as long as the money you have in the bank isn't owed to the IRS for last quarter's 941 taxes.

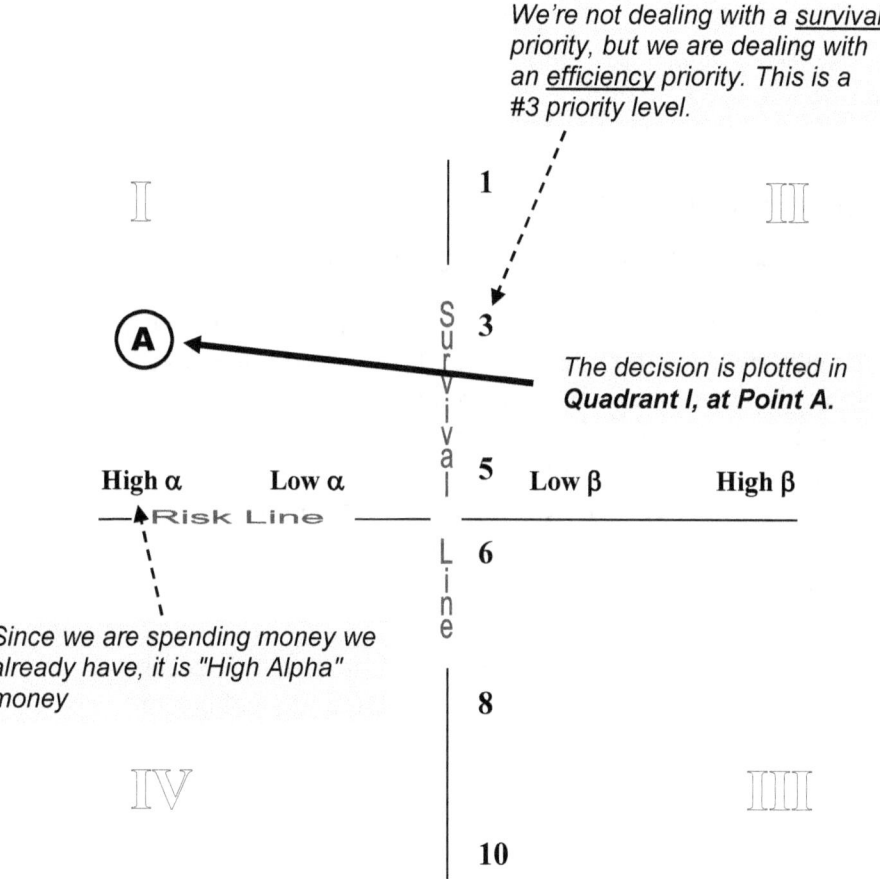

We're not dealing with a *survival* priority, but we are dealing with an *efficiency* priority. This is a #3 priority level.

I

III

1

S
u
r
v
i
v
a
l

3

The decision is plotted in **Quadrant I, at Point A.**

(A)

High α        Low α

5    Low β        High β

Risk Line

L
i
n
e

6

Since we are spending money we already have, it is "High Alpha" money

8

IV

IIII

10

**Spending Example 2:**

**Buying a new copier. Same Story, Different Verse**

Now, suppose your copier sales person convinces you that you actually need a copier that will handle your work load even when you <u>double</u> your present business level. Not only has your priority changed (now you're spending money in preparation of substantial growth), the cost of your copier doubled as well. But you're not worried. There is a $1500 check in the mail and you will have it by the middle of next week, so you go ahead and spend the money.

---

**NOTICE** that the same basic decision got "riskier" because the money isn't in hand yet and because the product is more than what the business needs right now.

---

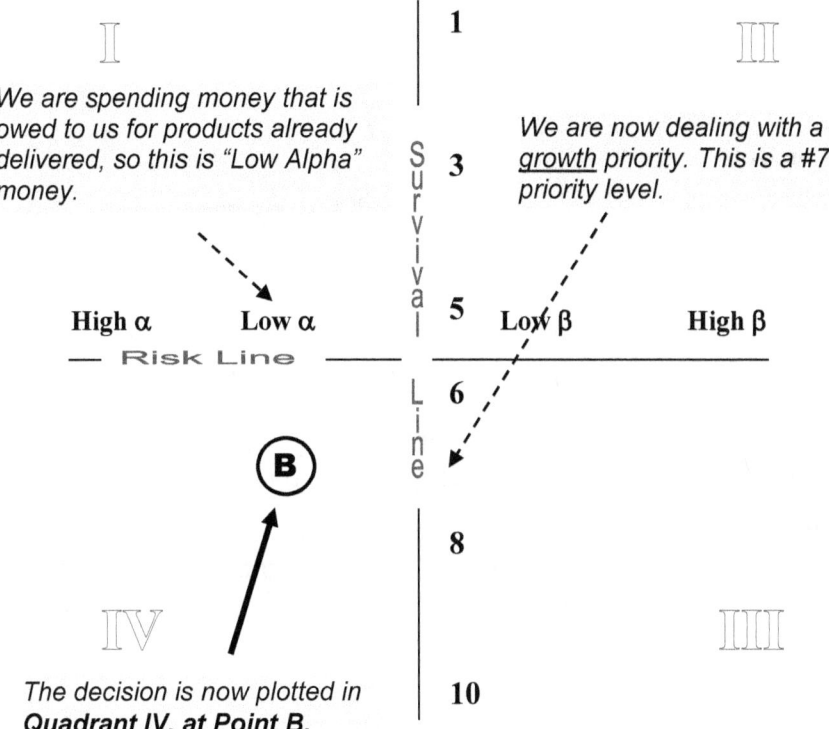

I

*We are spending money that is owed to us for products already delivered, so this is "Low Alpha" money.*

1

3

Survival Line

We are now dealing with a *growth* priority. This is a #7 priority level.

High α          Low α

— Risk Line ——

5   Low β          High β

6

B

8

IV

IIII

*The decision is now plotted in* **Quadrant IV, at Point B.**

10

**Spending Example 3:**

**Buying a new copier just got REALLY dangerous.**

If you really want to live dangerously, you let yourself get talked into buying a copier that folds, collates, edits, prints in three colors and does two sides at once, PLUS has its own 2,000 sheet paper deck for those really big jobs you're going to run when you start doing your own direct mail pieces. Woo Hoo!

This super copier costs $8,000, but you can get a nice 5-year lease for only $157.00 a month. With those immortal words "It will pay for itself in only 18 months" ringing in your ears, you sign on the dotted line.

Pay Attention To Why You Are Spending Your Money

I                                    1                    III

                                  S
                                  u    3
                                  r
                                  v
                                  i
                                  v
                                  a
High α        Low α               l    5   Low β          High β
— Risk Line ——

                                  L    6   *The decision is now plotted in*
                                  i        ***Quadrant III, at Point C.***
*If you succumb to the*           n
*"BS" logic of all that,*         e
*you are now dealing*                      *Welcome to*
*with a #8 priority level.*            8   ***ALLIGATOR***           ©
                                           ***ALLEY!***

IV                                                        III

                                       10

## SOURCES OF POWER

## THE INFERIOR POWERS

The common denominator of the Inferior Powers is that they require some type of external structure in order for them to have any influence. The structure itself can be either a physical environment, or a set of rules and procedures that we are *expected* to adhere to. In many cases, we are *required* to adhere to them.

Outside the particular structure that they represent, the sources of power virtually cease to exist. Consequently, the Inferior Powers can never be a source of enduring influence in and of themselves. They can only influence people who are "inside" the structure.

People will "follow" those who possess Inferior Powers only to the degree that it serves their ego or self interest. Once liberated from the influence of these powers (i.e., when we no longer need what the power provides), they cease to have any attraction for us.

For example, if you have a business that provides a necessary product and your business is the only supplier, you do not have to be too concerned about customer service or quality. But as soon as another source becomes available, your customers are "liberated" from your structure and they will cease to do business with you.

The designation "inferior" does not mean "inconsequential". While the Inferior Powers may not reach very far outside the structure, they can be very pervasive and dominant within that structure. "Inferior" refers to piety of the power, not the significance of it.

### Situational Power

Situational Power is limited to an individual or group having some measure of control in very precise situations. For example, a postal clerk when you need to send a package; a security guard at the airport until you pass through their checkpoint; a judge hearing your case in court; a secretary who puts a call through or approves an expense request.

Situational Power *can* instill a sense of loyalty from those in the situation. For example, your loyalty to a particular waiter is certainly present for you when you are visiting his restaurant, and sometimes it can even influence how often you visit that restaurant. Most of the time the that loyalty is probably not even in your conscious mind. But when you are going out to dinner, it is front and center.

One aspect of Situational Power is that it can be almost absolute in the relevant situation. Consequently, the holder of that power can be seduced by his importance, which often leads to an attitude of indifference or egotism. The high level of control in that situation is the main reason we tend to tolerate the person who has this power even when we don't like or respect them.

## Titular

This source of power is based on a "title", such as "Head Coach", "President", "Judge", etc. The degree of power is limited to the level of importance people place on that particular title. Titles infer a certain level of competence, character and authority. As such, they can assert significant influence over the community or organization from which the title is bestowed.

Quite often, especially in organizations, titles serve to reward someone or elevate prestige by designating a high level of competence. We all respond to hearing someone is a "*Senior* something", or "*Certified* something". Because titles do carry the weight of influence within a particular culture, they can be quite effective sources of power.

The amount of influence associated with Titular Power is dictated by the amount of importance a particular title has. In a very structured environment such as the military, the rank (title) of an officer invokes almost absolute loyalty, though people outside the military may have no loyalty whatsoever. The title of "Doctor" or "Minister" carries a much broader loyalty because society as a whole places a premium on them.

The influence of Titular Power is defined by two things:

1. <u>The level of obedience required for that title.</u> In our example of the military, it is of the utmost importance that the title be honored, or the entire system breaks down. In a court of law, the absolute power of the judge dictates absolute obedience. On the other hand, the title of "teacher" may carry no durability at all if the school does not enforce obedience.

2. <u>The level of competence demonstrated by the person holding the title</u>. Even in such absolute environments as the military or courts of law, incompetence can erode the level of power dramatically. Conversely, the power of the title of "teacher" can be exponentially enhanced by competence.

## Authoritative

This is the most controversial source of power because it is based in the power to <u>punish or reward</u>. In a business setting, that is a very potent kind of influence. Business exists in the world of success and failure, and the ability to reward those who do what you want and punish those who don't is a huge advantage.

One of the reasons that the previous power we discussed - Titular Power - is as influential as it is comes from the belief that someone with a "title" has the ability to reward and punish, at least in some circumstances.

Authoritative Power is potentially the most constructive <u>and</u> the most tyrannical of all the powers. When driven by honor and fairness, Authoritative Power promotes initiative and responsibility. But when it is driven by ego and self-interest it results in favoritism, abuse and corruption. Unfortunately, the line between the two is often blurred.

Authoritative Power commands loyalty in direct proportion to how dependant a person is on the reward or the avoidance of the punishment. If you have the power to fire someone, or promote them, you have tremendous power over that person.

But if they quit or get a different boss, your power disappears.

Keep in mind, this power derives its influence from the needs and self-interest of those who are controlled by it. The greater the magnitude of reward and punishment, the more likely this power is *to subjugate an individual's core values*. For example, if you really need to keep your job, you are much more likely to do things in that job that you don't like or even approve of.

The sheer magnitude of the power to reward and punish is also the source of its danger and mischief. The corrupt exercise of this power can reduce the people to their most primitive survival instincts, even causing betrayal and suppression.

> *"He who controls many, must fear many"*
> *Aristotle*

## A Final Observation About The Inferior Powers

Many of the Inferior Powers co-exist with other powers. For example, it is pretty typical to find a person who has Titular Power also having Consistent Power or Expert/Reverent Power. When that is the case, the exercise of the Inferior Powers tends to be more pragmatic and compromising

But when one of the Inferior Powers is the sole power a person has (or believes that is the only power they have) the exercise of those powers can become less flexible and even putative.

This tends to occur because the power itself is so tenuous. It relies on the existing structure to keep itself in place. Holders of these types of power tend to be more rigid in their commitment to the structure, even when it is not serving the most people.

Also, most people will use whatever power they have. And they will tend to use it at its maximum level when ever possible.

If you are making an agreement that is defined by one of the Inferior Powers, be prepared to adhere to tighter guidelines than if the agreement is defined by one of the Superior Powers.

## THE SUPERIOR POWERS

A compelling aspect of all the Superior Powers is that they have no formal structure. They exist outside the realm of protocol and ritual. As a result, they cannot be bestowed on a person, or removed from a person. Unlike the Inferior Powers, which must be managed in order to maintain their influence, the Superior Powers don't require management, they just exist.

### Consistent/Dependable Power

*"The world is full of people living lives of quiet desperation, preferring the certainty of their misery to the misery of uncertainty."*

Henry David Thoreau

When Thoreau made that insightful observation about human nature, he was lamenting the fact that the majority of people

will put up with a remarkable amount of abuse and unpleasantness in an effort to keep life predictable, even if it is REALLY unpleasant.

We humans place a very high value on predictability. Too much in some cases, as Thoreau lamented. But the desire for predictability is a critical piece of most people's lives.

We insist on knowing what to expect. People will put up with a lot of guff as long as they know what to expect. This need for predictability is the reason that this is such a potent and relevant source of power and influence.

The absence of certainty creates tension and guardedness. When people take actions from a perspective of survival, or avoiding being blind-sided, they will not be innovative, creative or generative. In fact, uncertainty causes people to NOT take risks or do anything that will result in being caught off guard. Their energy becomes invested in trying to anticipate and avoid upsets or inconsistencies.

Any time you can provide certainty, you are creating a space people want to be in. Whether it is knowing that their coffee will be good, or that their check will be on time, people ARE going to swarm to this source of power.

## Expert/Reverent

This power comes from having a level of information, talent and experience that is highly regarded in a particular environment. It can be very narrowly exercised (like the employee that knows EVERYTHING about setting up mobile e-mail accounts), or it can be broadly exercised, such as with a wilderness survival expert who knows EVERYTHING about hunting, fishing, making fire, setting broken bones with sticks and getting rescued.

It is always limited by the need for the information or expertise in a particular environment. But within that environment, it is enormously important.

More than ever before in our history, we have become a society that craves more information. And we will rely on almost any source if we think it is telling us the real deal. The source of up-to-date and accurate information is a real find. Moths to a light bulb is a fitting metaphor.

In a business, if you can be that source of information, you have a significant edge regardless of the industry. If you need to rely on another party who has that information, treat them well!

## Causative

A good example of Causative Power is the winning coach who is able to extract a high level of output from a championship team. The coach may have many of the other powers we've already discussed, but the leader who can "cause" others to take action will achieve a level of results that are not explained by the other powers.

Causative Power results in people taking an action for a reason that may or may not be in their self-interest, but they still believe is the best thing to do. It draws its strength and direction from each person's internal set of goals, standards and values.

The significance of Causative Power is that it often doesn't require any traditional structures to keep it in place. Existing structures, such as a business, team or even a municipality can help focus and reinforce Causative Power, but unlike the Inferior Powers, it can still exist even if the structure is removed.

## Charismatic (Invisible)

This is the most durable and commanding type of power. It is the power that has the greatest potential to influence large numbers of people. When Charismatic Power is at work, it triggers great enthusiasm and devotion.

Examples of charismatic leaders we have all heard about are Jesus Christ, George Washington, Abraham Lincoln and Martin Luther King. John F. Kennedy was said to have the ability to inspire even his adversaries into taking actions he wanted.

The biggest difference between Causative and Charismatic power is that Causative Power can be ignited by an external source, but it is driven by our own standards and values. We are in the service of what *we believe* are high standards and noble results. Charismatic Power, on the other hand, derives its influence from the special energy of another individual. When we are driven by that power we are in the service of that persons standards and ideals.

Not all charismatic leaders are good things. Adolf Hitler and Charles Manson were a couple of charismatic leaders that dwelled in the dark side of human nature.

Finding a truly charismatic leader in a business environment is a rare thing. But they do exist. One celebrated example is Steve Jobs, the founder of Apple. The key word that applies to all charismatic leaders is "visionary". If you do encounter one, be prepared to be confused at times. And impressed.

www.ingramcontent.com/pod-product-compliance
Lightning Source LLC
Chambersburg PA
CBHW051918170526
45168CB00001B/443